ANGELS AND THE ANGEL OF LIGHT

Grampa Ed

PublishAmerica
Baltimore

© 2013 by Grampa Ed.
All rights reserved. No part of this book may be reproduced, stored in a retrieval system or transmitted in any form or by any means without the prior written permission of the publishers, except by a reviewer who may quote brief passages in a review to be printed in a newspaper, magazine or journal.

First printing

PublishAmerica has allowed this work to remain exactly as the author intended, verbatim, without editorial input.

Softcover 9781629075228
PUBLISHED BY PUBLISHAMERICA, LLLP
www.publishamerica.com
Baltimore

Printed in the United States of America

A Book to Help **You** in Studying "**Your**" Bible
(Or may be used as a **group** Bible Study Book)
(Also a Book for Your Enjoyment)
NOTE: The Author only uses the King James Version Bible

The comments made in this book are the authors and the authors only, and is not meant to hurt anyone or anybody. He is sorry if he has offended anyone, at any time, while reading this book. This book is written by a "layperson" for a layperson trying to make their journey through the Bible much easier and friendly, while learning another Item from the Bible, such as angels.

I dedicate this book to all the people in the world who know God and his only begotten son, Jesus Christ. Also to those who are searching for God and Jesus, right now. God loves you, and so do I.

Grampa Ed

INTRODUCTION TO THIS BOOK: "ANGELS AND THE ANGEL OF LIGHT."

This small book, I pray, will teach you more of the Bible and the angels that are in the Bible. We will be going through the Bible, book by book, and looking for and studying all the angels listed. Also what their purpose's are, for you to understand, and I will try to make it enjoyable and easy to read. And will list the meaning of some of the words I think people may have trouble understanding. Also I will add a few jokes and quotes to make the journey a little friendlier. (The authors though are unknown, and I wish to thank them for their effort in making someone smile.)

Four other books written by Grampa Ed:
I must tell you though that these books have not had a lot of proof reading and I know now after re-reading them that a lot of mistakes have been found, but only grammatically and in spelling. This book I have taken a lot longer to do and I have checked a lot better. The four books are still good to read, but you may find a mistake here or there, and the publishers were not great at catching them, and one even charged me so much a word to check it. Oh well, live and learn.

<u>Does Your Flame Flicker?</u>—To help <u>you</u> get into and start reading the Bible and covers many items that are in the Bible. Author also has included some jokes and stories to make your journey easier. He also has listed a short synopsis of each

book of the Bible, so it will make it easier when you start to study the bible.

Afraid to Read the Bible?—To help you when you first start reading the Bible and covers many interesting items that are in the Bible. Included are some of the scientific items that are in the Bible and it took us (the people of earth) hundreds and hundreds of years to find them. Here is just one example; In Jonah 2:6 it mentions mountains of the ocean, yet man did not find mountains until they started diving into the depths and finding mountain ranges, then they found the Mariana's trench. Now they have found volcanoes at the bottom of the oceans. I believe that there are more than one hundred scientific items in the Bible.

Abishag—The Half Wife—(Christian but is X rated). Going after the un-churched to try to get them to read and study the Bible. A true story from the bible, but Abishag's story of her living along with other concubines with two kings, is fiction. A factual story from the Bible, but some of it is her story and is fiction.

The Seventy Seventh Day—Christian but is XXX rated {by the author}. This is when Satan takes over the world and what he does with a "Christian family." The book does contain a lot of sexual details, as the author again is going after those that only read sex novels, and is praying that it will lead them to the Bible. Two children (one girl and one boy) of the Christian family actually become prostitutes for Satan as he recruits' them into his religious concept. The third child goes to heaven without dying, for God calls her to him.

_____
_____

NOTE: WHILE YOU ARE READING THIS BOOK, YOU WILL NOTICE THAT I HAVE ADDED OTHER WORDS AND I AM NOT TRYING TO SAY OR TELL SOME OF YOU, THAT YOU ARE NOT SMART; WHAT I AM SAYING IS THAT OVER THE YEARS THAT I HAVE TAUGHT, I HAVE FOUND PEOPLE THAT "DO" HAVE PROBLEMS KNOWING WHAT A WORD MEANS, SO AS I WRITE, I DO PUT OTHER WORDS BEHIND (OR AHEAD) OF THE WORDS, THAT WILL TELL THEM, HOPEFULLLY, WHAT THE WORD IS IN TODAYS LANGUAGE. FOR I KNOW SOME PEOPLE MAY HAVE TROUBLE WITH THESE WORDS, WRITTEN IN THIS BOOK, THAT ARE ACTUALLY FROM THE BIBLE, INCLUDING ME. SO PLEASE DO NOT TAKE OFFENSE, I DO NOT WANT YOU TO BE ANGRY, OR RESENT ME.—THANK YOU.

NOTE: Leaders of Group Studies.

If you are going to use this book as a group study book, I recommend taking your time reading and studying your Bible. For I have found as I taught the Bible, that a lot of people do not know the Bible, the words confuse them, and if you go too fast they are lost, but most will not say anything to you about going at the speed you are teaching. A lot of people need someone to lead them, especially with the Bible. The most important thing to remember is that most people trying to study the Bible are blue collar workers, some with very little college, and some with a high school education only, and some without a lot of education. The others are a little of everything, including those that have been, or are, scared of reading the Bible.

A verse from the Bible to start us off:
PSALM 91:11-12 (KJV)
For He (God) shall give his angels over thee (you),
To keep thee in all thy ways,
They shall bear thee up in their hands,
Lest thou dash (smash) thou foot against a stone.

CHAPTER ONE

ANGELS OF THE BIBLE
TYPES OF ANGELS AND THEIR RANKINGS

To start with: the Bible I use is the King James Version, so if you are using another Bible, it may "not" be worded the same. I believe the KJV to be the most accurate Bible; yes, it is harder to read and understand, for it is in the Old English language, and the newer versions of the Bible have changed considerably over the years. The English language we use today and some of the meanings have changed in different Bibles, then, different people have also put in their own definition of items in their Bible. The problem here, that I see, is one word can make a big difference in the meaning of that particular sentence or paragraph. Yes, I do have trouble myself trying to decipher (or understanding) a passage, and when I do, I look in one of my other twelve Bibles, or my Bible Dictionary, or use my computer, and I have gone to the library to find some meaning of a word or verse. If you go to the library and need help, the librarian should be able to point you in the right section to look for your problem verse. (I am sorry to say, not always though).

We will start with the first book of the Bible, Genesis; and "humans" are **not** made first, as everything else was made before us. In Genesis two, verse two (Genesis 2:2) it reads, "Thus the heavens and the earth were finished and all the HOST of them."

Now some scholars believe that the word HOST to be the first mention of angels, along with myself, except I am not a scholar, just self taught. When I looked up the word HOST, it mentions that angels are those who attend and worship God. Another passage says that they are messengers of God, and are normally not seen by us, the people of earth. They have been reported as being seen, many times, over the years and also in the Bible that goes way, way back in history, and there will be many types of angels. Yes, I do believe we all have a guardian angel and some people keep their angel "very busy".

There are a lot of books out there about angels helping people, but some, I read with a question mark over my head, as some are very hard to believe and I wonder if they are really true stories. Someday maybe I will get to meet an angel, or just see one, but I am not going to hold my breath until I do see or meet one. I do believe I was helped by someone or something a couple of times, but I cannot say it was an angel nor would I swear it was not an angel.

Before we go any further, I wanted to mention this: Some scholars believe that "angels were here before the earth was formed" and I try to tell people to read Genesis two, verse two. Some scholars go with Job, chapter thirty eight (38), verses four through seven (4-7), and to tell you the truth I have read this and just do not see what they are talking about. Now some of these scholars claim that it covers angels and stars, moon, sun, deity, and the persecuted (wronged) people of God. If we have not been on earth yet, how did the persecuted people get their? That is why I go with Genesis. I will let you look both of these verses up in both books of the Bible, and read it and let you decide for yourself.

I know, you want to know what "deity" means, I should let "you" look it up, but I am not that mean. Some scholars say it means God. (Some say God the Father, the Son, and the Holy Ghost, which is what I go by). Some say it means God and/or other beings regarded as divine.

A definition of an angel is; "a spiritual (supernatural or heavenly) being, created by God to serve him." They are created slightly higher than humans, but they "do not marry", "have children", "and do not die". Some have fallen out of grace with God and now spend eternity in chains while others are free to oppose the works of God along with the head "fallen angel", Lucifer. (He is otherwise known as; Satan, or the Devil, or Angel of Light, plus many other names that people have called him). He also was an archangel at one time.

A lot of scholars view the subject of angels as being very difficult as there is so little to go by in the Bible and elsewhere. Most of the time when the angels are mentioned, it seems to inform us about God, or what will happen to others or ourselves for not following God's commandments. Sometimes the angels give us directions on what to do, but you may only have a feeling in your heart, or in your mind. An example of this: A man was getting ready for bed, when he was getting this urge to go help an elderly woman two houses from his. He quickly got dressed again, and headed for her house and when he got there, he saw flames coming out from under the roof. He broke the door down and pulled her out to safety, then called the fire department. The elderly woman told him that she asked God for help moments before he broke the door down, and she thinks it was her guardian angel that told her neighbor to come to her aid. It very well could have been, and there are many stories out their similar in nature to this one. Have you ever had a feeling to do something, and you actually ended up helping someone?

In the Bible, (depending on which Bible you use) it mentions angels around two hundred and ninety up to around three hundred times, using the entire Bible. In the Old Testament they are mentioned around one hundred sixteen times and in the New Testament angels are mentioned around one hundred seventy five times. In the sixty six books of the Bible we use today, angels are listed in thirty four books. Some day, when I have nothing to do, (Sure) I will count them for you and myself. But I am retired and very busy (And tired), and if you believe that, well, I just might have a bridge to sell you.

If you read other books on angels, which can be interesting reading, do not believe all you read as some stories are manmade for the amusement of man. Now I am talking about the books that say this angel did this for me, etc…I am saying you can believe what is in the Bible, or if written by some scholarly persons. Did you notice I said SOME scholarly persons; I say this because some have preached that angels are with "them" and then usually ask for money. Just do "NOT" worship angels, this I will talk on later. One other item I want to mention; all the angels were created at one time which is tens of thousands times tens of thousands, and are innumerable. It mentions in Jeremiah 33:22 (KJV) that: "As the host of heaven cannot be numbered, neither the sands of the sea be measured".

There have been debates between scholars about the rankings of angels that are in the Bible, and what the ranks pertain too. I will try to list them and tell you a little about them before we go into the Bible. Just try to remember some of it, so as you read your Bible, you can decide what group the angel, or type of angel it is, in the verse you are reading.

Now some scholars will say "ranks of angels" and others will go with "tiers of angels" while others will say "choir of angels", as to myself I prefer "ranks of angels".

The only thing listed in the Bible, that I can see, is more of what type the angel is, like Cherubim, or an Archangel, etc:. After many years with the Bible I still am uncertain of what RANK the angel is, so I guess I have to study some more to set myself straight. At least most angels do not have a name that we on earth know, God probably has names for them but we do not know them, except for the names of the archangels. (If you have a lot of time you can go to the library ad look up angels or get on the web and do the same and you will find a **lot** of literature on angels, and to me I think some of it should be taken off the web as it is very untrustworthy.)

I have found a few books out there with a name for an angel, but they are not from the bible. One book taken out of the Bible as being not reliable centuries ago—The Book of Enoch, does list many angels by name, but most of them seem to be fallen angels. I must leave that one up to the scholars to figure out. For it is beyond my expertise. (I know someone wants to know what "expertise" is: It is knowledge).

The following is a list of the rankings of angels done by a bishop in Milan (northern Italy) around the fourth century, by the name of St. Ambrose. He listed nine rankings of angels, in this order.

Seraphim
Cherubim
Dominions
Thrones
Principalities
Powers
Virtues

Archangels
Angels

As you noticed, St. Ambrose put the archangels lower than seven other ranks. Then an unknown author around five hundred A.D. wrote that there were nine choirs of angels, divided into three groups of hierarchy (or rankings). This is how he listed them:

The first group or sphere you have: <u>Seraphim, Cherubim, and Thrones</u>.

The second group or sphere you have: <u>Dominions, Virtues, Power</u>.

The third group or sphere you have: <u>Principalities, Archangels, Angels</u>.

Again the Archangels and Angels are listed near the end of the groups or spheres. Now the only thing I can think of why they did this is, the way they thought, meaning the groups should be written from the bottom up (or read from the bottom up). Otherwise maybe they just put them in this order, because others did so before them. Now in another book by a well known preacher of our day, and I found elsewhere while I was reading on angels, they are listed in this manner and it is the one I go by:

Archangels
Angels (also some watchers)
Seraphim
Cherubim
Principalities
Authorities
Powers
Thrones
Might
Dominion

Now this list there are ten ranks of angels and for a long time I scratched my head over this, until one day I was studying the Bible and right in front of me the word <u>Might</u> came to my vision. It was right in front of me many times and I just missed reading it. How many times I have missed it and never realized it, which is why I keep telling people to re-read the Bible for you will miss something, and maybe more than one time. I could remember seeing Might, but not as an angel, then, I found it mentioned once in <u>Ephesians 1:21</u> and I think I have found it elsewhere, but old age will not let me remember, but I WILL find it and let you know where it is. It is good to write notes if you are studying the Bible. You will need them later.

Then I came across one everyone has forgotten; <u>"Rulers"</u> and you can find it in <u>Colossians 1:16</u> and the definition I found pertaining to Rulers; they are angels that rule heaven under God, doing his work and making sure everything is done correctly. I will talk a little more on a couple of items I found in Revelation when we get there, pertaining to types of angels.

So I am saying there are "*<u>eleven</u>*" types of angels instead of nine or ten with maybe two more when we talk about them later in this book. (I am already wondering how many scholars of the Bible will say I am wrong, "and" I might have stepped on somebody's toes.) Oh well, that's life.

Also, did they include "watchers"? When I count, I do not think they did, so it could be up to "*Twelve*". If they included watchers, they at least should have mentioned it.

In the following paragraphs I will try to give you simple definitions of each angel so it will be easy for you to understand.

<u>ARCHANGELS:</u> They are the head angel or first angel over the other angels. How many archangels are their? Well

I know of four, but in literature I have found maybe seven angels listed as archangels. Two are special angels who are mediators between God and the people on earth. The names of them are Michael and Gabriel; the other two are Raphael and Uriel (also called Sariel). The other names I believe you could find in the lost book of Enoch. I will not go into them at this time so not to confuse you.

ANGELS: There are a lot of definitions pertaining to angels, but I will try to keep it short. They are a spiritual being, being primarily a messenger of God. They have no names that we know of, and one angel says in the Bible, that "their names are secret". I do believe that God does have names for them, but for his use, not ours. Without a name you also will have a hard time trying to worship an angel.

WATCHERS: Just another name for an angel, or agent of God, a messenger. Now some scholars say they are fallen angels, but I do not believe that all of them are fallen for I have found some that are still with God when you read everything in the Bible. Yes, some of them lusted after human women and had sex with them and the women gave birth to giants. At first I thought this was contrary to what I have learned, as angels cannot have children. Then someplace I read that they used the bodies of men to accomplish their feat of pleasure and God banned them from heaven. Just be careful when you read and then decide which of the watchers are bad or good.

SERAPHIM: Heavenly beings that were seen by Isaiah, and according to him, they shine like fire, or brighter, and have six wings. Two wings are for covering their face (Lest they look directly at God), two wings are for covering their feet and lower body, with two wings for flying. Some scholars say they are serpentine in shape and shiny skin, which gives us "Flying fiery seraphs". (Or serpents) So they may be more

Mythological (imaginary) than heavenly beings, with some scholars saying they are angels.

CHERUBIMS: Heavenly beings that guard "with flaming swords", this is what God put by the Garden of Eden to guard the "Tree of Life". They also flank and guard the "Throne of God." A few scholars say they support God's throne, (or hold up the throne) but I believe they guard the throne. Now Ezekiel also saw them in a vision, but as four winged, four faced, accompanied by whirling wheels and support the platform that supports God's throne. But are they cherubim's or another type of angel? If they are another type then we may have "thirteen" types of angels, but I will let the scholars decide on that. You as readers may make up your own mind to that question.

A lot of people think this is one of the first mentions of UFO's and they throw it in everybody's face. But to me, how did they get into a vision (or dream) and how would UFO's be in heaven? You will find this in many books if you are into UFO's or are studying UFO's.

Just remember that "Baby" angels are not listed in the Bible "anywhere", so all the drawings of baby angels on cards for Valentine's Day and other places are strictly man made.

The following is a list of angels that a few scholars say they could be, or, are believed to be evil angels. Now I want you to NOTE that some scholars have them listed as working for God, and I have read an article (a very long time ago) that I will try to remember, giving a small definition of what these groups of angels are:

PRINCIPALITIES: They direct the lower angels and are entrusted with the management of the universe. There is a lot more that they do, and I would believe you could find this out by looking up on a computer, or maybe at a library. When you read later they will be classified as evil angels also in the Bible. It is up to the scholars to decide which is which. I go with some evil, some good.

AUTHORITIES: or the virtues (merits). They work miracles and send down the grace of miracle-working to those worthy of such grace, so they may work miracles.

THRONES: In them God intellectually resides. They serve God's justice, glorifying it and pouring out the power of justice onto the thrones of earthly judges, kings and masters to bring the right judgment.

POWERS: They have the power over the devil, to restrain the demons and to repulse the temptations brought upon the people by the demons. They also help those wrestling with passions and vices to keep out evil thoughts. Again, these angels are also listed as evil angels in the Bible, as you will read and study later and this will be for the scholars to decide what is what. I myself will go with half evil, and half good.

DOMINION: They dominate (rule, govern) the rest of the angels, and send down power for prudent governing and wise management to authorities on the earth. Again there is much more but you should look it up and see what else they may do.

This could be their ranking, but a lot more work and studying by scholars to prove it to us all would be needed. Those that work for Satan are usually called demons and will oppose God however they can, but God is using some of them for his benefit, which we do not know why at this time. God is allowing this to happen until the second coming of Christ. Now you can study these angels by looking them up in a Bible dictionary, on the computer, or in a library.

Now I know that someone, someplace, will say this is wrong and will give a different definition for all of these listed above. Why do I say this; it may be your church you go to and the pastor has his say of what they are, or someone thinks they know better than the scholars. I have found a couple of different items listing some of these as being fallen angels, but I am going to stick with what I have put down as the definition, per some of the scholars, that I have read.

One item I read was (the one I like) that when Jesus died on the cross, he made all these angels or demons defeated and "no longer" effective, but only if you have God and his son Jesus in your heart. If you fail to believe in Jesus then these fallen angels (or demons) will be around to help you to fail in many things.

NAMES OF ARCHANGELS AND OTHER TYPES OF ANGELS:

The following are names of archangels, along with other names for the type of angel that I think you should know as you read your Bible, so you know who they are and who is good or evil.

MICHAEL: A prince or archangel mentioned in the Bible by name only, and is also a chief prince. You will find this in Daniel when you read that book of the Bible. He argued with Satan over the body of Moses (Found in the book of Jude). Michael is the commander of the heavenly angels (or army of angels). Michael also pushed Satan and his followers out of heaven for God, and has always been victorious over Satan, and of course Michael is a good angel.

GABRIEL: One of the archangels found in the Old Testament, and also known as the "Man of God". Gabriel is the interpreter of visions and mysteries. He is also the archangel that oversees the Garden of Eden, cherubim's, and serpents, and also was sent in judgment over the children born of fallen angels. Now some scholars debate this (having children), as how an angel that never marries can have children, but Satan and his followers always find ways to fight God and do many things that should not be done. I was not their when this happened (neither was you) but I could just see it happening. We will never know for sure tell it either happens again, or when we go to heaven and can find out up there. Gabriel is also the angel that told of the birth of John the Baptist, and the birth of Jesus, to Mary, and of course Gabriel is a good angel.

ABADDON: This is the angel that speaks along with death (Book of Job) and rules over swarms of deadly locusts which have plagued humans in the past and may come again in the future. He also rules over the bottomless pit (Hell) where those that do not repent go. (Book of Revelation) Abaddon is a good angel with a very hard job for he must do the will of God over humans. See Apollyon in the next verse, as these two names are actually the same, except one is Greek and the other is Latin. Some scholars have problems with these two as some believe them to be bad angels and others believe them to be good angels.

APOLLYON: (Also see Abaddon)—This name appears once in the New Testament and some scholars believe it to mean "the angel of the bottomless pit" (Hell). He is the angel of destruction and pestilence, (destructive, quick moving disease, similar to the plaque) and the king of the bottomless pit. Some scholars believe him to be the antichrist (just before Satan comes to rule the earth), and others believe he is just an angel doing God's work, and that he holds the key to the bottomless pit. You really have to study Revelation in the Bible to find out about him (or them). But DO NOT STUDY the Book of Revelation without FIRST studying all the rest of the Bible, or you will be lost. Now I am going out on a limb here and say these two are good angels and work for God, just do not make them angry though as they could also work for Satan, when and if, he needs them.

DESTROYER: This angel is called the "Angel of Death" and under God's orders performs as a destroyer. We will find this angel in about eight books of the Bible. You may remember him best as the angel that takes the life of every new born child of the Egyptians, when Moses is trying to get the Israeli people out of Egypt. The Israeli people were told to smear lambs blood on their door frames so the angel would not take any Israeli child, only those of the Egyptians. I do have a hard time saying he is a good angel, but he is, and just does the work for God.

SATAN: I could probably write a book on this fallen angel, but I will try to keep it small but interesting but yet understandable. Satan is called by many names and I will list a few of them here. You may have heard these names before and you may also have your own name for him. The names are; Devil, Azazel, Mastema, Beelzebub, Sammael, Belial, (or Beliar) the Evil One, Ruler of the Demons, the Enemy, Ruler of the World, Tempter, and the "Angel of Light." You will find the Angel of Light in the book, <u>Second Corinthians</u>.

There is more than one item that mentions what Satan wants to do, and one of those is to get people away from God and to worship Satan, or idols that Satan wants you to worship. He also has a desire, from some literature I have read, to kill as many humans that are believers of God that he can. I imagine, depending on what type of Christian you are and how strong your belief is. Denominations play no role in his desires; we are all on his list. Satan is the best known of the fallen angels and is presumed to be the leader of the fallen angels; he is always there, tempting all of us to sin.

DEMONS: Evil spirits, or evil angels, fallen angels, are all agents of the Devil with their jobs being; to oppose the work of God and his people. They can occupy a mind or a complete human body and can cause terrible problems, for anyone they can get into. The Book of Tobit, which is recognized in the Catholic, Greek and Russian Orthodox churches, but is not recognized in the other churches and is considered one of the Apocryphal books, (Not trustworthy by the English and American Bible Societies), and contain many acts of demonic spirits. Demons possess (or get into the bodies of men) and had sex with human women and created giants as you will read in the Bible elsewhere. "They themselves cannot have children so they must possess a human body." I do not think I have to tell you what type of angel they are, but it is a four letter word spelled EVIL.

SONS OF GOD: This refers to all angels that worship God and do his bidding.

SON OF GOD: This refers to only one person; God's only son Jesus Christ.

MALE OR FEMALE ANGELS? : In Zechariah one of the passages refers to an angel as being a female. Just remember that they are invisible spirits and "probably can take on any form they wish". Nowhere does it say they are roly-poly babies that you see on Christmas cards, Valentine cards, etc: They are always listed as grown up angels.

WINGS ON ANGELS: Now some scholars say that there are passages in the Bible that depict angels with wings, some flying, some are not flying. Some of the angels do not have wings and some scholars think that the angels radiate so much light around them, it just looks like wings and could be called a large halo, covering about one third of their body. I will just have to wait and see them for myself before I can say which is which. Maybe there are angels that have wings and others that do not have wings, which would bring the total types of angels up one more. I will let the scholars debate that one. Of course if there are two types of cherubim's then it would be up to, maybe, fourteen.

UNUSUAL FEATURES OF ANGELS: As you read different passages in the Bible you will find some angels will have unusual features as listed in the Book of Daniel. Daniel saw an angel that had arms and legs of polished metal with precious stones and a face like lightning. The following are a few items to remember as you read.

"Always remember", angels were created by God, for God, to minister to him, then if needed they will minister to us on earth. They are created above us but "DO NOT" worship them, for angels are NOT gods. Only worship God and his only son Jesus Christ.

In the Book of Matthew, Jesus taught of angel's existence more than once.

Angels "ARE" personal beings.

Angels have "INTELLECT" which is mentioned in Matthew and in First Peter.

Angels have "WILL" as told in the Book of Jude.

Angels have "EMOTIONS" which is mentioned in both books, Job and Luke.

Now in Psalm 104 verse three, it talks of "WINDS", (Who walks on the wings of the wind), and some scholars believe this refers to angels. I have read this Psalm a few times and it does refer to God and the things he has accomplished here on earth, but nowhere have I found that it says or refers to angels. (Not the King James Version that I use anyway) All I see is that it refers to those that "walk on the wings of the wind". I did find where there is a strong wind that comes through the house, but it brings the Holy Ghost. Now I suppose it could be angels, but I will leave that one to the scholars to decide and let all of us know for sure, what is what. You may decide for yourself on that one, but I am going to leave it to the scholars.

This is a list of things that angels are to do, which we find as we read the Bible.

They <u>Praise and Worship</u>.
They are <u>Revealing</u>.
They are <u>Guiding</u>.
They are <u>Providing</u>.
They are <u>Protecting</u>.
They are <u>Delivering</u>.
They are <u>Strengthening</u>.
They are <u>Encouraging</u>.
They <u>Answer Prayer</u>.
And at death, they are <u>Caring</u> for "believers".

This is the simplest way of what angels can and will do that I can come up with: Hopefully you will understand their role a little better with the short definitions above.

Items pertaining to Satan to show his existence: Seven Old Testament books and all the New Testament books refer to Satan. Also, Jesus told of his existence, in the Books of Matthew and Luke.

NOTE: I will be having you look up verses and read them or this book would get very large and then maybe boring, which is not what I want. I want it to be an exciting read for you and something you can understand. If you do not have a Bible, you should buy one, or borrow one from someone close to you, and maybe your church would lend you one. Just get one you feel comfortable with, and it is not from some occult organization. You can find many Bibles on the internet, or in book stores (the larger the store, the more they will have), and in Christian book stores. There is one site on the internet (and they do send catalogs out also) that I do like; it is www.Christianbook.com, and they do have sales going on all the time. It is a good site to check out, and of course you have www.barnesandnoble.com and www.amazon.com plus others too many to mention. Although I do enjoy going to the small independent book stores and Christian book stores, then as you shop you know what the Bible looks like, feels like, readability, type print, etc;.

SPIRIT: This is not an angel, but a spirit is many things and I would think it could be the same category as an angel. Confusing, yes it is. But just read on and I will try to explain this. In the New Testament it would be worded as God's Spirit and if you are living in the spirit you would enjoy the fruits of love, peace, kindness, patience, self control, etc…It can mean a direct contact with a divine person like an angel, or God himself, or his only begotten son Jesus. It can ALSO mean an evil or unclean spirit who under God's orders carries out a negative aspect of God's will. "Then" there are those that have left God and work for Satan doing the most hideous of works against the people on earth. (I hope you understood this.) It's like a two sided coin, with both sides being heads.

THIS IS WHAT WE AS BELIEVERS OF GOD AND HIS ONLY BEGOTTON SON, JESUS CHRIST, <u>MUST DEFEND OURSELVES FROM AT ALL TIMES:
SATAN AND HIS EVIL SPIRITS.</u>

NOTE: Now before we go into the different books of the Bible, please take your Bible out (and dust it off) then follow along with what I have written, for I have not typed everything into this book, and if I had I would not finish this book until a month after they called my name up above. Then I would have a hard time getting it published. (From the grave, that is.)

All <u>Italicized words</u> are "directly" from the King James Version Bible, and <u>Italicized and Bold print</u> are "words of angels". All other words in normal print are the authors, or are items about the King James Bible. <u>Red Print, Italicized</u> will be "words of Jesus"; and <u>Black Underlined, Bold, and Italicized</u> words are "God's words".

For your information: In the Books of Enoch (one of the Lost Books of the Bible, for they are not trustworthy) there are names I believe of "twenty one" angels, if I remember correctly. This is the only book that I know of that has the names of angels listed in it, and some day I will have to study all the lost books of the Bible to see if other books list angels names as well. Of course if you are interested, "YOU" could study them and let me know, Thanks. (I am getting slower in my old age.)

I will start in the Bible with the Book of Genesis and will go through the Old Testament first, and then we will go through the New Testament, studying only the good angels. Then when we are finished we will come back to Genesis and go through the Bible one more time studying Satan and his angels. That will give you a chance to REALLY understand you're Bible, do not worry it is not that long and will actually be easy if you follow me. If I can do it, anybody can do it.

Quote:—While we are sleeping, angels have conversations with our souls.

<u>Dear God letters from kids,</u>

Dear God,
I bet it is hard for you to love everybody on earth, there are only four people in my family and I can never do it.—Dan

Dear God,
Of all the people that work for you, I like Noah and Samson the best.—Don

Dear God, My brothers told me about being born, but it does not sound right. They are kidding, aren't they?—Becky

CHAPTER TWO

GOOD ANGELS OF THE OLD TESTAMENT
THE BOOK OF GENESIS
THEME: THE BEGINNINGS

Before we start, I want to mention two items found in the Bible, which I believe you should really read and follow:

Acts 8:30—*Understandeth thou what thou readest.*

I hope you do not need a translation for this as I am not giving it to you. Sorry, you will just have to figure it out for yourself.

And the next one is:

Galatians 3:24—*Wherefore the law was our schoolmaster to bring us unto Christ, that we may be justified by faith.*

To me this is saying that we must know the laws of the Old Testament to understand the New Testament. For the Old Testament was our schoolmaster and if we do not understand all of the books in the Old Testament, we will have a hard time with the New Testament.

I will also give you a small definition of what each book is about, just prior to starting that book, some will be small paragraphs and some will be larger paragraphs:

This book (Genesis) is about how God created the heavens and earth, Adam and Eve, and how sin started. Then it goes into the life of Noah, Abraham, Isaac, and Jacob, ending with the life of Joseph.

We have already covered Genesis 2:1 at the beginning of this book and I do not like to repeat items, for then you would get bored before we get too far. So I am going to skip it here, if you need to, just go back and read it. Thanks.

GENESIS 3:24—(This is after Adam and Eve were chased out of the Garden of Eden).

So he drove out the man, and he placed at the east of the Garden of Eden, <u>Cherubim</u>, and a flaming sword which turned every way, to keep the way of the tree of life.

This is one place in the Bible that tells us what type of angel was used. And as it says the angel is a Cherubim, a good angel. This is after Adam and Eve tasted the fruit from the tree of knowledge, of good and evil, so God chased them out of the garden for doing what they had been told NOT to do. They were tempted by a serpent (snake), and God made the serpent eat dust by crawling on its stomach, for all generations. (Taking the serpents' legs away.) To this day people are still looking for the Garden of Eden, but no one has found it yet. Some say they know, but it is under water and they cannot get to it. Of course I do not want to meet the angel with the flaming sword, so I am going to stay away. (So I am a little afraid of swords, then have it be a flaming one also, no thanks).

GENESIS 16:7—(This is after Sarah was very stern with her maid Hagar, for Abraham was going to have a child with her, to keep his name alive, as Sarah was barren {cannot have children} and is getting too old to have children).

And the <u>angel</u> of the Lord found her by a fountain of water in the wilderness, by the fountain on the way to Shur. (Shur is a desert region in Sinai and could have been a major caravan route to Egypt) *And he said,* **Hagar, Sarah's Maid, whence** (where) **camest** (come) **thou? And whither** (where) **wilt thou go?** *And she said, I flee from the face of my mistress*

Sarah. And the <u>angel</u> of the Lord said unto her, **Return to thy mistress and submit** (surrender) ***thyself under her hands. And the*** <u>***angel***</u> ***of the Lord said unto her, I will multiply thy seed exceedingly, that it shall not be numbered for multitude.*** (In other words, you will have many children, and they will have many children, too many to count.) *And the* <u>angel</u> *of the Lord said unto her,* ***behold, thou art with a child, and shalt bear a son, and shalt call his name Ishmael; because the Lord hath heard thy affliction*** (distress). ***And he will be a wild man; his hand will be against every man, and every man's hand against him; and he shalt dwell in the presence of all his brethren.*** (Family or brothers).

There is no rank listed for this angel, but the way it is worded, I believe the angel to just be a messenger of God, and a good angel. Now you should read other verses before what I have listed, as well as a few after what I have listed, to understand what is going on in that story.

According to literature and the Bible, Ishmael is considered to be Arabic and his portion of his inheritance was the land from the "River of Egypt to the Euphrates." (Euphrates is also a river.) All the children of Ishmael are considered to be Muslims.

GENESIS 18:2—(This part of Genesis explains that the Lord and two angels came into Abrahams camp, and the Lord and Abraham have a discussion about Sodom and Gomorrah, with Abraham questioning the Lord about destroying the cities; if there are ten or more people that are not sinful with the Lord agreeing with Abraham.) {The angels depart and head for Sodom, with the Lord leaving later.} For the continuation of this story we will read Geneses 19 which is below.

NOTE: Even though these angels destroy, they are considered to be good angels, and I believe these to be called

"Destroyer Angels", and are just doing what God has them do. There are people out there that cannot understand why God does this so much in the Old Testament. But just think, if you made a cake and it tasted terrible, you would throw it out, would you not. This is just what God is doing, he made people and they just do what they want and break every commandment there is, just as though there is no God. The people just keep on sinning and breaking all laws, so he starts over. (Now this is the way which "I think" God may be doing, you may have your own ideas.) And of course there will be scholars yelling at me over this.

GENESIS 19:1—(This tells of the angels coming into Sodom and finding Lot, [Abrahams nephew] and Lot talks the angels into staying at his home for the night as Sodom is dangerous during the night hours.) The people of the city come to Lot's home seeking the strangers "to do wrong" with them, (Having sex with men) and started to do wrong with Lot, but the angels pulled Lot into his own home and caused blindness for those, that want to sin, outside the door of Lots home.

Now, I want YOU to read your Bible very slowly and understand what is written before you go any farther. If you do not understand something, please ask your pastor or a Bible group leader, or look it up on the computer or in a book, or at the library, and then go on when you have your answer and understand what is written—PLEASE. Why? Too many people keep reading their Bible without understanding what they read, "then they get lost and quit reading".

GENESIS 19:12—*And the* men (Angels) *said unto Lot:* **Hast thou any here besides?** (Is anyone else here?) **Son in laws, and thy sons, and thy daughters and whatsoever thou hast in the city, bring them out of this place: For we will** *destroy this place, because the "cry of them waxen great"* (Becomes Louder) *before the face of the Lord; and the Lord has sent us to destroy it.*

Remember people, the King James Version Bible is written in the old English language, so there may be words that will throw you, so look them up and when you find the definition, re-read the sentence. Thanks.

GENESIS 19:15—*And when the morning arose, then the <u>angels</u> hastened Lot, saying,* **Arise take thy wife, and thy two daughters, which are here; lest thou be consumed** (Destroyed) *in the iniquity* (Immoral acts) *of the city. And while he lingered, the <u>men</u> (Angels) laid hold upon his hand, and upon the hand of his wife, and upon the hand of his two daughters; the Lord being merciful unto him; and they brought him forth, and set him without* (Outside) *the city. And it came to pass, when they had brought them forth abroad,* (Away from ones home, or outside the city) *that <u>he</u> (Angel) said.* **Escape for thy life; look not behind thee, neither stay thou in the plain; escape to the mountain, lest thou be consumed.**

Lot then talks the angel into allowing him and his family to escape to a small city near there.

GENESIS 19:21—*And <u>he</u> (Angel) said unto him.* **See, I have accepted thee concerning this also, that I will not overthrow this city, for which thou has spoken. Hast thee; escape thither;** (To the farthest side) **for I cannot do anything till thou be come thither.**

Lot's wife could not resist looking back, and turned into a pillar of salt. Then Lot left the little city of Zoar and dwelt in a cave on the mountain with his two daughters and the daughters feared that no other man was alive to be their husbands, so they got their father drunk and slept with him, both daughters became pregnant by their own father, and both having sons.

I do believe that one of these angels is a Destroyer angel (Or an angel of death), but both of them could be. The other one could be a Cherubim, maybe. I think I will stay with both being Destroyer angels.

GENESIS 22:11—We now jump to Abraham and an angel. Now this can be confusing as a lot of people think that Abraham was talking with God, but as you read you will see that it does say "The Angel of the Lord".

And the "angel of the Lord" called unto him out of heaven, and said; **Abraham:** *and he said, "Here am I". And he said (angel),* **Lay not thine** *(your)* **hand upon the lad, neither do thou anything unto him, for now I know that thou fearest** *(fear)* **God, seeing thou has not withheld thy son, thine** *(your)* **only son from me.**

Then out of the blue, Abraham found a Ram caught in some thicket by its horns, so Abraham offered the Ram instead of his son for his sacrifice.

GENESIS 22; 15—*And the angel of the Lord called unto Abraham out of heaven a second time, and said,* **By myself have I sworn, saith** *(Says)* **the Lord, for because thou hast done this thing, and has not withheld thy son, thine** *(your)* **only son: That in blessing I will bless thee. And in multiplying I will multiply thy seed as the stars of the heaven and the sand which is upon the nations of the earth be blessed; because thou has obeyed my voice.**

In this verse, "it is the angel delivering the message from God through the angel's voice", and God allowed Abraham and his wife Sarah to have children (seed) even at an old age. Then those children will have many children and on and on until there are more than the stars in heaven, and the sands of earth.

It does not list what type of angel this is and if it was an archangel I would think there would be a name, so I am going to say it was a captain of one of the ranks of angels, a messenger angel but high up on the list of angels.

GENESIS 24:7 AND 40—Angels are only mentioned in this verse, but the angels do nothing and do not say anything. Just look up the verse and read it and see what you think of the verse. Remember I use the King James Version Bible so yours may say it differently than mine.

GENESIS 28:12—This is when Jacob was starting to look for a wife in the land of his mother and tarried (stayed) all night at one place and took a stone for a pillow and slept, and then had a dream. This is how it is worded in my Bible:

And he dreamed, and behold a ladder set up on the earth, and the top of it reached the heaven; and behold the angels of God ascending and descending on it. And behold the Lord stood above it, and said, **I am the Lord God of Abraham thy father, and the God of Isaac; the land whereon thou liest, to thee will I give it, and thy seed.** (Seed here means, to all of your children, grandchildren, and great grandchildren and so forth.)

There is more that God says to Jacob, but I will not go into all of that, as I want to keep this more on the angels of the Bible. When you do read all of it, you will see there are more angels but are only visible to Jacob in his dream, they do not speak, and God speaks for himself.

GENESIS 32:1—To really understand this story, you should read all of chapters 31, 32, and 33. This is another story about Jacob and the chapter (31) will tell you that Jacob found a woman to marry,(but not the oldest daughter in the family) but her father made him work for her hand, then refused Jacob for his oldest daughter had not found a husband. So Jacob worked longer for her hand, but also worked for cattle, sheep, camels, etc...Finally Jacob got his bride and was off to find some land, and was afraid his brother would come after him for he had stole the first born rights by cheating his father into believing he was the first born. (With the help of his mother).—Now there is not a lot about angels in these verses, but just keep reading anyway, for the story is a very good story and will help you learn the Bible.

And Jacob went on his way, and the <u>angels</u> of the Lord met him. And when Jacob saw them, he said; This is God's host; and he called the name of the place Mahanaim. (This is a place that is unknown, but is believed to be in Gad along the border with Manasseh).

How many angels, no one knows, and Jacob does say "THEM", so it had to be more than one. Jacob takes his servants and all his animals and possessions and divides them into two groups for he is afraid of what his brother may do, when they meet. He then sends his wives and children and their servants across a brook and they were left alone. Now in the next part it will tell us of Jacob wrestling someone all night and this person threw Jacobs thigh out of place by just putting his hand on the thigh. But Jacob would not stop wrestling this person unless this person would bless him. So this person blessed Jacob and changed Jacobs name to Israel. Now Jacob thinks he wrestled God all night, but no one has seen God's face, so did he really see God? I do not think so: I think he wrestled with an archangel or a captain of an angel group. God would not have wrestled all night and I do not think an archangel would wrestle all night, so I am going with a captain of a group of angels. Others will disagree with me, but that is okay with me, that's what makes the world go around and around.

Quote:—If we were all like angels, the world would be a heavenly place.

Dear God kids jokes.

Dear God, If we come back as something, please do not let me be my sister, because I hate her.—Peggy

Dear God, My brother is a rat, you should give him a tail, then everyone would know he is.—Paul

(And my favorite) Dear God,

I want to be just like my daddy when I grow up, but not with all that hair all over him.—Jenifer

CHAPTER THREE

GOOD ANGELS OF THE OLD TESTAMENT
BOOKS OF EXODUS, LEVITICUS, DEUTERONOMY, JOSHUA, JUDGES, RUTH

The Book of Exodus
<u>The Theme of this book of Exodus is: God's redemption of Israel</u>

This book is about multiplying Abraham's descendents into a great nation and taking them, with Moses as their leader, out of Egypt. The Ten Commandments and other laws were given to the people from God through Moses. Moses also led the Israelites in building the first tabernacle.

<u>EXODUS 3:2</u>—This is during the time when Moses went to the mountain of God with his sheep and as he was there, he was visited by an angel. Again a lot of people think that this was all God but as you read it does say an angel of the Lord, then later God speaks to Moses.

And the <u>angel</u> of the Lord appeared to him (Moses) *in a flame of fire out of the midst of a bush; and he* (Moses) *looked and behold, the bush burned with fire, and the bush was <u>not</u> consumed.*

Then when Moses went to look at the bush, God spoke to him from the bush and told him, that he was on holy ground. Moses hid his face, for he was afraid to look upon God. At this point Moses followed the word of the Lord and brought the people out of Egypt. Now this angel I believe to be a captain of a group of angels, because if it was an archangel I would think a name would be given. I do believe it to be more than a messenger angel. I do hope you saw were the angel of the Lord first spoke to Moses, "then" God spoke to him.

EXODUS 14:19—This part of the story is when Moses is leading the people away from Egypt with the Pharaoh from Egypt, chasing him with his troops.

And the <u>angel</u> of God, which went before the camp of Israel, removed (or switched places) *and went behind them; and the pillar of the cloud went from before their face, and stood behind them. And it came between the camp of the Egyptians and the camp of Israel; and it was a cloud of darkness to them* (Egyptians) *but it gave light by night to these;* (Israeli people) *so that the one came not near the other all the night.*

As you noted, I hope, that the cloud kept the Egyptians from finding the people of Israel; this is just before they crossed the Red Sea. To really learn this story, do not be afraid to read the whole book of Exodus. Now this angel I believe is more than a messenger angel, maybe another captain of a group of angels and again no name is given so I do not believe it is an archangel. But (and that is a big word) when you read all of Exodus 23:20 you may think he is an archangel. Then as you read you will notice there is no name given to this angel so I do not believe it to be an archangel. This angel could be a Cherubim but one high up the ladder.

EXODUS 23:20—This is during the time that "god is giving Moses" the Laws of Justice and he tells Moses;

<u>Behold, I send an angel before thee, to keep thee in the way, and to bring thee into the place which I have prepared. Beware of him, and obey his voice, provoke him not; for he will not pardon your transgressions,</u> (The committing of acts that violate a law, command, or moral code)**<u> for my name is</u>**

in him. But if thou shalt indeed obey his voice, and do all that I speak; then I will be an enemy unto thine enemies, and an adversary (enemy, foe) *unto all thine adversararies. For mine angel shall go before thee in unto the Amorites, and the Hittites, and the Perizizites, and the Canaanites, the Hivites, and Jebusites, and I will cut them off.*

I do hope as you read that no name is given for this angel, but with what God is telling Moses that he (and the people) HAS to obey him, so he has to be a powerful angel. So I believe him to be a captain of a group of angels and maybe even a destroyer angel, for he will not pardon the people under Moses, for their transgressions (Breaking God's laws and instructions). Remember THIS IS "GOD" telling Moses—and it is not an angel speaking.

EXODUS 32:34—This is just after the time when Aaron made a golden calf to worship, for the people wanted it. For they feared Moses had led them astray and the Lord spoke to Moses saying:

Therefore now go, lead the people unto the place I have spoken unto thee; behold mine angel shall go before thee; nevertheless in the day when I visit I will visit (Not forget) *their sin upon them. And the Lord plagued the people, because they made a calf, which Aaron made.*

Again THIS is God speaking to Moses, not an angel, and do you remember which of the Ten Commandments the people broke? Is there more than one commandment broken? If you cannot remember look up Exodus 20 and read it. (I know, you do not have the time to do that so I will tell you, but do not be so lazy, look it up. "Do not make a graven image" and "Thou shall have no other God's before me"; see that was easy, was it not?) The angel that is talked about in this verse I believe to be just a messenger angel, but could be a captain of a group of angels, which I lean toward. How about you? Do you think it is a messenger or a captain?

EXODUS 33:2—Here God is again speaking to Moses and tells him to depart from the land that they are in, and instructs Moses as such:

And I will send an angel before thee, and I will drive out the Canaanites, the Amorite, and the Hittite, and the Perizite, the Hivite, and the Jebusite: Unto the land flowing with milk and honey.

As you noticed, I hope; that again this is God talking about an angel leading the people, and the angel does not talk to Moses. Is this angel a Cherubim, or just a messenger angel? I know I have thought before that the angel was a captain of a group of angels, but the more I think on it I just may go with a Cherubim, but I will let you decide on this one.

The book of Leviticus

The theme of this book is: Holiness and worship.

God instructs Moses to tell the people about worship, sacrifices, offerings, feasts, and holy days and God also expects his people to be holy, but provides atonement (punishment) for sin.

LEVITICUS—There are No angels listed in this book of the bible that I know of, if I did miss one just blame it on old age—MINE.

The Book of Numbers
The theme of this book is: Wandering in the wilderness.
In this book it tells of God who will not permit disobedience and causes the people of Israel to wander for forty years.

NUMBERS 20:16—Here, as Moses and the people of Israel are on their way through the kingdom of Edom, and have asked the king to allow them to pass through his country, but he would not allow it. (Now this just mentions an angel only). Moses is telling the king that:

And when we cried unto the Lord, he heard our voice and sent an <u>angel,</u> and has brought us forth out of Egypt; and behold, we are in Kadesh, a city in the uttermost of thy border.

Still the king would not let them through his kingdom, so Moses had to take the people all the way around this kingdom of Edom. Please read this entire chapter to understand what the Bible has to say about this. It will also tell of the death of Miriam, Moses' sister, and at the end of the last chapter it will tell of the death of Aaron, Moses' brother.

NUMBERS 22:22-35—Here the king of Moab (Name of Balak), is frightened of the Israel people and sends for a prophet named Balaam and wants Balaam to curse the people of Israel, so they do not come into his land. God tells Balaam not to go with Balak's messengers but he does anyway, and God is angry at Balaam. Starting at verse 22 it reads:

And God's anger was kindled because he went: and the <u>angel</u> of the Lord stood in the way for an adversary (To change his direction or to stop him; a foe or enemy) *against him. Now he was riding upon his ass, and two servants were with him. And the ass saw the <u>angel</u> of the Lord standing in the way, and his sword drawn in his hand; and the ass turned aside out of the way, and went into a field: and Balaam smote* (struck) *the ass, to turn her into the way. But the <u>angel</u> of the Lord stood in* *the path of the vineyards, a wall being on this side, and a wall on that side. And when the ass saw the <u>angel</u> of the Lord, she thrust herself into the wall, and crushed Balaam's foot against the wall; and he smote* (struck) *her again. And the <u>angel</u> of the Lord went further, and stood in a narrow place, where was no way to turn either to the right hand or to the left. And when the ass saw the <u>angel</u> of the Lord, she fell down under Balaam: and Balaam's anger was kindled and he smote* (struck) *the ass with a staff. And the Lord opened the mouth of the ass, and she said unto Balaam, "What have I done unto thee that thou hast smitten* (struck) *me these three times?" And Balaam said unto the ass, "Because thou has mocked me: I would there have a sword in my hand I would kill you." And the ass said to Balaam, Am I not thine ass, upon which has ridden ever since I was thine unto this day? Was I ever wont to do so unto thee? And he said Nay* (No)*. Then the Lord opened the eyes of Balaam, and he saw the <u>angel</u> of the Lord standing in the way, and his sword drawn in his hand: and he bowed down his head, and fell on his face. And the <u>angel</u> of the Lord said unto him;* **Wherefore** (what reason) **hast thou smitten** (struck) **thine ass these three times? Behold, I went out to withstand** (Stop or change your mind) **thee, because thy way is perverse** (wrong) **before me. And turned from me these three times: unless she had turned from me, surely now also I had slain thee, and saved her alive.** *And Balaam said unto the <u>angel</u> of the Lord, I have sinned; for I knew not thou stoodest in the way against me; now therefore, if it displease thee, I will get back again. And the <u>angel</u> of the Lord said unto Balaam:* **Go with the men but only the word that I shall speak unto thee, that thou shalt speak.** *So Balaam went with the princes of Balak.*

Now this time it is the angel talking and I hope you remembered what type of angel it is. If not, go back and look at the different definitions of angels. If you said it was a Cherubim you are right.

The Book of Deuteronomy
The theme of this book is: Renewal of the covenant.
This book is about the second laws, reviewing the first four books and the Ten Commandments. A call to love and obey God; with blessings for those who are obedient and curses for disobedience. It pertains to the death of Moses and selecting Joshua as the new leader.

DEUTERONOMY 33:2—Now in this verse there are some scholars that say this pertains to angels, but others say no. We have a slight difference here between the Old Testament and the New Testament. In the New Testament a Saint would be a Saint and nothing else as far as I am concerned, but in the Old Testament a saint is a person of God, which I suppose you, could stretch into an angel. Just open your bible to this verse and read it, then YOU make the decision. After reading this verse a few times, trying to decipher it, I have decided it means saints and only saints, and not angels, so I will go against those that say they are angels. Remember though I am not a scholar, and at my age I do not think I want to go back to school. Oh to be young again, and do what we should have done years ago, but wishful thinking gets a person nowhere.

The Book of Joshua
The theme of this book is: Faith in God brings victory.
This book tells of Joshua who won many victories and who tells the people to remain faithful to God, and to obey God's law. Then God divides the land into twelve sections, one for each tribe. You have to really pay attention to which tribe gets what as one tribe will only be priests and they do not get land. This book is a good one to take notes on. Actually, I would prefer if you wrote down notes in a separate notebook, instead of highlighting or underlining items in you Bible, especially if you have spent good money on one, as a good Bible should last you a lifetime. You may want to pass it down to someone later in your life.

JOSHUA 5:13-15—This is just before Joshua had the priests and the warriors of Israel march around and around Jericho before the walls came tumbling down. This is the way it is worded in the King James Version Bible of mine.

And it came to pass, when Joshua was by Jericho, that he lifted up his eyes and looked, and behold there a <u>man</u> (angel) over against him with a sword drawn in his hand; and Joshua went with him, and said unto him, Art thou for us, or for our adversaries? (Enemies) *And he said,* **Nay; but as <u>captain of the host of the Lord</u> am I know come.** *And Joshua fell on his face to the earth, and did worship, and said unto him. What saith my Lord unto his servant? And the <u>Captain</u> of the Lord's host said unto Joshua.* **Loose** (take) **thy shoe from off thy foot: for the place whereon you stand is holy,** *and Joshua did so.*

Here the angel identifies himself as a Captain of the host of the Lord, and did you see that Joshua worshiped him, or did he worship the Lord and only asked the angel what God wants him to do. Here is one point you have to be careful, when you read too fast, you will automatically think he worshiped the angel, but the way it is worded I do believe he worship the Lord and then asked the angel what God wanted him to do, and only that. Also the angel had a sword, so I believe him to be a <u>captain of the cherubim's</u>.

_____

_____

_____

The Book of Judges
<u>The theme of this book is:Rebellion brings defeat.</u>
In this book the people promise to keep the covenant, but again turned from God and started worshiping other gods. They did what was right in their own eyes, so God sent a foreign power and opposed them. The Israelites cried for deliverance and God rose up a deliverer for them.

<u>JUDGES 2:1-4</u>—This is during the time that Joshua is leading the people from Egypt to the Promised Land, but they do not obey the Lord and left the Amorites in their land, and Israel did not take it for their own land. (Then right after this, in verse eight, it tells of Joshua dying, for none of the original people will be left to settle in the new land per God, for their past sins.) The angel is speaking FOR the Lord: *And an <u>angel of the Lord came up from Gilgal to Bochim and said;</u>* **I made you to go up out of Egypt, and brought you unto the land which I sware** (swore) **unto your fathers; and I said, I will never break my covenant with you. And you shall make no league** (covenant) **with the inhabitants of this land; ye shall throw** (knock) **down their alters; but ye have not obeyed my voice: why have you done this? Wherefore I also said, I will not drive them out from before you; but "they shall be thorns in your sides, and their gods shall be a snare** (trap for the unwary) **unto you".** *And it come to pass, when the <u>angel of the</u>*

Lord spake (spoke) *these words unto all the children of Israel, that the people lifted up their voice and wept.*

This has been going on from day one when the people of Israel left Egypt, they obey God for so long and then sin, then they cried out as God punishes them over and over. It seems as, the Israel people, never learn what is what. If you are having problems, are you listening to God; or yourself, or someone that is leading you astray? Did you notice that the angel is speaking to the people for God, as God does not want to talk to them anymore, and I do believe this to be still going on in that area of the world; they are still trying to get the Israeli people out of their land, as they call it.

JUDGES 6:11-22—This is during a time that Israel was being punished by the Lord for not obeying him and the Midianites were taking what they want from the people of Israel. He sent an angel unto Gideon, who claims that he is not worthy to do what the Lord wants. Now it is a little confusing slightly as Gideon calls the angel Lord, but as you read it, you will realize that it is an angel of the Lord. I know there will be some scholar out there that will disagree with me, but that is the way I READ IT. The Lord docs talk to Gideon, after the angel leaves, when Gideon is worried he might die for looking at an angel: *And there came an <u>angel</u> of the Lord, and sat under an oak which was in Ophrah, that pertained unto Joash the Abiezrite: and his son Gideon threshed wheat by the winepress, to hide from the Midianites. And the <u>angel</u> of the Lord appeared unto him, and said unto him.* **The Lord is with thee, thou mighty man of valour.** (Courage) *And Gideon said unto him, O my Lord, if the Lord be with us, why then has all this befallen us? And where be all the miracles which our forefathers told us: Did not the Lord bring us up out of Egypt? But now the Lord has forsaken us, and delivered us into the* hands of the Midianites. And the Lord looked upon him, and said. (Remember this is the angel talking FOR the Lord.) **Go in this thy might** (strength) **and thou shalt save Israel from the hands of the Midianites.** And he (Gideon) said unto him, Oh my Lord, wherewith shall I save Israel? Behold my family is poor in Manasseh, and I am the least in my father's house. And the Lord said unto him, **Surely I will be with thee, and thou shalt smite the Midianites as one man.** And he (Gideon) said unto him, if now I have found grace in thy sight, then shew me a sign that thou talkest with me. Depart not hence, I pray thee, until I come unto thee, and bring forth my present (offering), and set it before thee. And he <u>(angel)</u> said, **I will tarry** (wait; linger) **until thou come again.** And Gideon went in, and made ready a kid (goat), and unleavened cakes of an ephah (one third to two thirds of a bushel) of flour; the flesh he put in a basket, and he put the broth in a pot, and brought it out under the oak, and presented it. And the <u>angel</u> of God said unto him, **Take the flesh and the unleavened cakes, and lay them upon this rock, and poor out the broth.** And he did so. Then the <u>angel</u> of the Lord put forth the end of the staff that was in his hand, and touched the flesh and the unleavened cakes; and there rose up fire out of the rock, and consumed the flesh and the unleavened cakes. Then the <u>angel</u> of the Lord departed out of sight. And when Gideon perceived that he was an <u>angel</u> of the Lord said. Alas O Lord God! For because I have seen an <u>angel</u> face to face.

Now it is my belief that this angel is more than just a messenger just delivering God's message to Gideon. I would say that it would be another captain or possibly an archangel, but since there is no name mentioned I am going with a captain of one of the groups of angels. Again if you do not keep your mind on what you read you could say Gideon was taking directly to God. Always take your time and study what you read.

JUDGES 13:3—At the beginning of this chapter, this is close to the end of the forty years of captivity of the Israel people by the Philistines; and there was a man that lived there by the name of Manoah and his wife who was barren. (No children) This is how it is worded in the King James Version Bible of mine:

And the <u>*angel*</u> *of the Lord appeared unto the woman, and said to her,* **Behold now, thow** (you) **art barren, and barest not; but thou shalt** (shall) **conceive, and bear a son. Now therefore beware, I pray thee, and drink not wine, or strong drink, and eat not any unclean thing: For, lo, thou shalt conceive and bear a son;** <u>**and no razor shall come on his head;**</u> (Underlined by this author) for **the child shall be a Nazarite unto God from the womb; and he shall begin to deliver Israel out of the hand of the Philistines.** *Then the woman came and told her husband saying, A man of God came unto me, and his countenance* (face) *was like a countenance of an* <u>*angel*</u> *of God, very terrible: but I asked him not whence he was,* (where he came from) *neither told me his name. But he said unto me, behold, thou shalt conceive, and bear a son; and now drink no wine nor strong drink, neither eat any unclean thing: for the child shall be a Nazorite to God from the womb to the day of his death. Then Manoah intreated* (begged) *the Lord and said, O my Lord, let the man* (<u>angel</u>) *of God which thou didst send come again unto us what we shall do unto the child that shall be born. And God hearkened to the voice of Manoah; and the* <u>*angel*</u> *of the Lord came again unto the woman as she sat in the field; but Manoah her husband was not with her. And the woman made hast, an ran, and shewed* (showed) *her husband, and said unto him. Behold, the man* hath appeared unto me, that came unto me the other day. And Manoah arose, and went after his wife, and came to the man, and said unto him, Art thou the man that spaketh (spoke) unto the woman? And he said **I am.** And Manoah said; now let thy words come to pass. How shall we order the child, and how shall we do unto him? And the <u>angel</u> of the Lord said unto Manoah, **Of all that I said unto the woman let her beware. She may not eat anything that cometh of the vine, neither drink wine or strong drink, nor eat any unclean thing; all that I command her let her observe.** And Manoah said unto the <u>angel</u> of the Lord, I pray thee, let us detain thee, until we shall have made ready a kid (goat) for thee. And the <u>angel</u> of the Lord said unto Manoah. **Though thou detain me, I will not eat of thy bread; and if you offer a burnt offering, thou must offer it unto the Lord.** For Manoah knew not that he was an <u>angel</u> of the Lord. And Manoah said unto the <u>angel</u> of the Lord, What is thy name, that when my sayings come to pass we may do you honor? And the <u>angel</u> of the Lord said unto him. **Why askest thou thus after my name, seeing it is secret?** So Manoah took a kid as a meat offering and offered it upon a rock unto the Lord: and the <u>angel</u> did wondrously; and Manoah and his wife looked on. For it came to pass, when the flame went up toward heaven from off the altar, that the <u>angel</u> of the Lord ascended in the flame of the altar. And Manoah and his wife looked on it, and fell on their faces to the ground. But the <u>angel</u> of the Lord did no more appear to Manoah and his wife. Then Manoah knew he was an <u>angel</u> of the Lord.

This child that was born to Manoah and his wife was named Samson, and do you remember what happened to him when the queen had his hair cut off—He lost his strength.

Also did you notice that the woman was never mentioned by name, only that she is childless and is the wife of Manoah.

Did you also notice that the <u>angel when asked his name</u> did not give it, for it is <u>"secret"</u>? Then mentions that the offering MUST be offered to the Lord, "not to an angel", and waited for Manoahs wife to bring her husband the second time he appeared. Now I do believe that this angel is just a messenger of the Lord, and nothing else for he did not burn the offering as before, but just rode the flame to heaven.

The Book of Ruth
<u>The theme of this book is: Love, devotion, and redemption.</u>
This book is about a young widow, who out of love for her mother-in-law has abandoned her own culture. Boaz, a relative of her dead husband, marries her. God accepted her, for she has accepted him. Even thought she was a Gentile. She also became an ancestor in the family tree of Jesus.

<u>RUTH</u>—In this book, there are no angels listed, but I would like you to read and study the book, and then prove me wrong. Do you know who Ruth is, and why she is mentioned? She is not an Israelite and "she is in the family tree of Jesus. Now prove me wrong by studying this book and going to the section that tells about Jesus family tree whom begat whom and look for her. I know that is so boring to read this begat material, but do you ever wonder about your family tree. If you know your family tree, how many people have you bored with it? Just remember it will be worth it to find and read about Jesus' family tree and the story of Ruth. (Some scholars say it is a love story and I lean that way myself).

I suppose I will have to tell some people as they will never find it. She is a Moabite and was "pagan" and left her heritage to follow the Jewish people and to worship the God of Israel. Then she married into the Israeli heritage by marring Boaz, becoming one of the people in the ancestral line of Jesus. You never know if God will use you someday so just watch your "P"s and "Q"s for God uses us all, for his work.

Quote:—Angels can fly directly into the heart of the matter.
—

Dear God letters by Children.

Dear God, If you watch me in church this Sunday, I will show you my new shoes—Danny

Dear God, I would like to live for 900 years, like that guy in the Bible, what's his name.—Larry

Dear God, On Christmas can I have a pony? I never asked for anything before. You can "look it up".—Bruce

Dear God, You do not have to watch me all the time now, cause when I cross the street, I look both ways.—Pete

CHAPTER FOUR

GOOD ANGELS OF THE OLD TESTAMENT BOOK'S OF 1ST AND 2ND SAMUEL, 1ST AND 2ND KINGS, 1ST AND 2ND CHRONICLES, EZRA, NEHEMIAH, ESTER, JOB.

The Book of 1st Samuel
<u>The Theme of this book is: Transition from judges to kings.</u>
This book is about Samuel who was a prophet, priest, and judge, but the people demanded a King. Then God, through Samuel the profit, anointed (picked) Saul as Israel's first King. Then Saul turned from God, and David was anointed king to succeed Saul. Saul, who was jealous of David, tried to kill him, but David fled. After Saul was killed in battle, David returns to be one of the greatest kings of Israel.

<u>1ST</u> SAMUEL—There are no angels listed in this book. (I do believe that I am in "big" trouble if there are angels listed)

_____
_____
_____

The Book of 2nd Samuel
<u>The theme of this book is: God blesses obedience.</u>
In this book it tells of David who extends Israel's border from roughly Egypt to the Euphrates, but then David sins. Both his kingdom and his family fall into disorder, with David's son leading a bloody revolt against David his father.

David, with prayer and repentance becomes a man after God's own heart. David has a lot of wives and concubines, and wrote many Psalms to God.

2ND SAMUEL 24:16, 17—In this chapter, King David broke a commandment of the Lord, not to number (or count) the people. King David had Joab go out into the country and count all the people, and when Joab returned and told King David, the king knew he had sinned and asked forgiveness. God sent the prophet Gad with three things he would do and that King David had to choose one of the three. King David chose the three day pestilence (epidemic of a disease) upon Israel and seventy thousand men died. This is when the angel is mentioned:

And when the <u>angel</u> stretched out his hand upon Jerusalem to destroy it, that the Lord repented him (David) *of the evil and said to the <u>angel</u> that destroyed the people,* **<u>It is enough, stay now thy hand.</u>** *And the <u>angel</u> of the Lord was by the threshing place of Araunah the Jebusite.*

Here King David built an altar, and had burnt sacrifices to the Lord and the Lord was entreated (forgiving) for the land, and the plaque was stayed (stopped) from Israel.

Now this angel should be a destroyer angel of the Lord, but is still a good angel. Sometimes it is hard to understand why someone could destroy and still be called a good angel in the Bible, but it is sort of like the military, you do as you are ordered. And all this angel was doing was following God's orders.

The Book of 1st Kings
<u>The theme of this book is: Division of the kingdom.</u>

In this book it tells of the death of King David and the reign of his son Solomon, who wrote a lot of Israel's literature. Solomon, who had many wives and married many foreign women which he had been told not to do by God, falls into many problems with the people and with God. This book also tells of the construction of the Temple in Jerusalem and the importance of worshiping properly. God also sends prophets but mainly Elijah, who told the people not to serve other god's.

1ST KINGS 19—Now in this chapter, Elijah had slain the profits of Baal, and Jezebel was going to kill Elijah.

This is how it is worded in my King James Version Bible.

Elijah fled and rested under a Juniper tree and asked the Lord to take his life as he was not better than his fathers. And as he lay and slept under the Juniper tree, behold an <u>angel</u> touched him. And said unto him, **Arise and eat.** *And he looked and, behold, there was a cake* (usually made from wheat or barley and may have figs or raisins in them, shaped like a ring or flat shaped) *baken in the coals, and a cruse* (jar) *of water at his head. And he did eat and drink, and laid him down again. And the <u>angel</u> of the Lord came a second time, and touched him, and said,* **Arise and eat; because the journey is too great for thee.** *And he arose, and did eat and drink, and went in the strength of that "meat"* (There is nothing above that says that it is meat, as he had cake and water. This could have been meal instead of meat but I did not decipher the Bible.) *forty days and forty nights unto Horeb the mount* (mountain) *of God.*

I just wish I could have a meal that I could eat and have enough strength to last forty days and forty nights. That's a little over a month without food. Maybe I could lose a few pounds around my "old" tummy. Of course I do not think an angel will ever feed me though, oh well. Of course this is a good angel and is probably just a messenger angel, doing what God has told him to do.

1ST KINGS 22:19—This verse has just a mention of angels when Jehoshaphat was talking to the king of Israel. This is how it is worded:

And he said, "Hear thou therefore the word of the Lord: I saw the Lord sitting on his throne, and all the <u>"host"</u> of heaven standing by him on his right hand and his left".

Now the way it is worded I do believe that "host" means **"all"** of the angels standing by him in heaven while God sits on his throne. Now I know some scholar or teacher, or somebody will probably say I am wrong, but this is a freedom of speech country and I do believe I am right.

The Book of 2nd Kings
<u>The theme of this book is: The results of disobedience.</u>

This book is about when Elijah's prophet ministry ends, and his successor Elisha starts. Also, Israel's disobedience causes their faithfulness to continue to go out of control. It tells how Israel (The Northern Kingdom) was defeated by the Assyrians with the Southern Kingdom, Judah, having more kings who try to attempt new reforms. Then the Southern Kingdom is defeated by the Babylonians and lastly Jerusalem falls, with the people exiled for seventy years in Babylon, which had been prophesized by Jeremiah.

2ND KINGS 1:3—The verse here is worded as such:

Ahaziah fell down and was sick and sent messengers to enquire of Baalzebub, the god of Ekron whether I shall recover from this disease. But the <u>angel</u> of the Lord said unto Elijah *the Tishbite,* ***Arise, go up to meet the messengers of the king of Samaria, and say unto them. Is it not because there is not a God in Israel, that you go to enquire of Baalzebub the god of Ekron? Now therefore thus saith the Lord, thou shalt not come down from that bed on which thou art gone up, but shalt surely die.*** And Elijah departed.

Then we go to chapter 1:15—*And the <u>angel</u> of the Lord said unto Elijah.* ***Go down with him, be not afraid of him.*** *And he arose, and went with him.*

Now I did not copy all of this, so you need to read this section to understand more of what is going on, right from 2nd Kings, chapter 1, verse 1.Then when you get to chapter 2 you will read of Elijah going to heaven in a whirlwind along with a chariot of fire and horses of fire which also parted Elijah from Elisha, the next prophet of Israel. Now pay attention to this—"Elijah went to heaven without dying". Yes I did say that, Elijah went to heaven without dying. This is the first mention of someone doing this, how many others did, no one knows, and I am at a loss for words, but if it can happen once, it can happen again.

Now this angel I believe to be just a messenger angel of God's and is a good angel.

2$^{\underline{ND}}$ KINGS 6:16-17—This verse is right after Elisha makes an axe head float on water and the king of Syria was angry at Elisha and had his horses and chariots come at night and circled the city were Elisha was staying. When Elisha's servant sees them in the morning, he asks Elisha what to do. This is how it is worded in my KJV Bible:

Fear not, for they that be with us are more than they be with them. Then Elisha prayed and said, Lord, I pray thee, open his eyes, that he may see. And the Lord opened the eyes of the young man; and he saw; and behold, the mountain was *full of <u>horses and chariots of fire</u>* (These are angels) *round about Elisha.*

Now in this verse it tells of angels, but none speak, it is just a description of the angels, and the way it is worded I would think they would have drawn swords with them also. Now reading this I automatically think of Cherubim's as the angels. All of them ready to do battle for Elisha.

Note:—Swords are the word of God, in angel's hands; they represent a spiritual function; they can also mean; salvation, peace, and truth.

Now I am hoping that I am keeping this book easy enough to understand and that you will continue to read and learn more of the Bible, which contain both God's word and of his only begotten son, Jesus Christ. If you still are having trouble understanding, then I think you should talk with your pastor or go to someone that is teaching, like in a small Bible study group.

2<u>ND</u> KINGS 19:35—This is when the king of Assyria is thinking of marching into Jerusalem and the Lord finds out and says he will not, for they only destroy everything in their wake. This is how it is worded in my Bible:

And it came to pass that night, that the <u>angel</u> of the Lord went out. And smote in the camp of the Assyrians an hundred fourscore and five thousand: and when they arose early in the morning, behold, they were all dead corpses.

Again, this only mentions an angel but also what the angel did during the night. Because he destroyed the army I am going to say he was a destroyer angel, following God's orders.

Note:—Before I go farther, I do want you to realize that angels are mentioned throughout the Bible, but in prayer from someone praying to God and will mention angels or will call one by rank, such as Cherubim's. Now some of these I may have missed;—forgive me if I do miss a couple here or there and we will blame it on very OLD age, mine.

The Book of 1st Chronicles

<u>The theme of this book is: God keeps the covenant.</u>

This book is about the history of the Southern Kingdom, Judah, stressing David's worshipping and the kingdom under him, and details the construction of the temple by Solomon. <u>NOTE:</u> When the First and Second Chronicles where written, it was all one book, then scholar's centuries ago divided this book into two books.

<u>1ST CHRONICLES 12:22</u>—Now in this part of the Bible, we have some scholars saying this is about angels while others say no. As I read it, it pertains to all the mighty men of valor from different tribes and is listed as hosts, which you will see when you read this verse. Yes it does say host, but as you read, it really is talking about the Hosts of God, not angels. This is how it is worded: Look for the word LIKE.

For at that time, day by day there came a great host, like the host of God.

Now did you notice the one little word in that sentence that really makes a difference—the word is LIKE. Did you read it? Then it goes on to list all the tribes and how many men were from each tribe. To me I would say that this is just a phrase to indicate that all together it was a great host of men, not angels. Although you can say that they can be deceased people, which have gone to heaven. Again, I know someone out there will disagree with me, but that is all right, and they can prove me wrong, that is better yet, for we learn something new every day of our lives, and I learn new things all the time.

<u>1ST CHRONICLES 21:15-16</u>—I am going to have you read this chapter and verses listed, for it is the same as what was in 2nd Samuel 24:16. The Bible does this every once in a while

and sometimes you learn a little more and other times you do not. Here the angel is a destroyer angel like it was before and yes, he is still classified a good angel.

Quit complaining and read it, or I will give you a surprise test along the way. I am a big Meany, am I not?

_____

_____

_____

The Book of 2nd Chronicles
The theme of this book is: The temple and worship.

This book pertains to the temple and worship, with the continuation of Israel's history from First Chronicles. It recalls the Power and Wisdom of Solomon and recalls the fall of Judah into sin.

2ND CHRONICLES 18:1—This is where Ahab, King of Israel has four hundred prophets and they all say to invade Ramoth-gilead to do battle and Ahab asks the King of Judah, (Both are kings of the divided kingdoms of Israel) Jehoshaphat, to go with him to do battle and he says he will if they seek the prophet Micaiah and see what he prophesies as he is a prophet of God. The King of Israel does not like Micaiah as he always prophesizes bad against him, but Micaiah says to do battle. The king (Ahab) was not sure because he always prophesizes bad for him. But Micaiah says he sees all of Israel scattered upon the mountains, as sheep that have no shepherd: and the Lord then says:

These have no master; let them return therefore every man to his house in peace. The king of Israel says see, he prophesizes against me. Micaiah says to the king, Therefore hear the word of the Lord; I saw the Lord sitting upon his *throne, and all the "<u>host of heaven</u>" (angels) standing on his right hand and on his left.*

Now the way it is worded, did God actually talk to them or just to Micaiah and then he passed it to the kings. Now I do believe it was told to the prophet and then he passed it on to the kings. Now this is all it says about the "hosts of heaven" and as you read it will switch to spirits and is called a lying spirit and will put lies in the mouths of the prophets, but does so with the "approval" of God. Then as you read farther you will see that Ahab, the King of Israel is killed in battle. Now again as you read you see the people continually go against God and he would punish them, and it is all through the Old Testament. Only God knows why he has kept the people of Israel, his people.

2<u>ND</u> CHRONICLES 32:21—In this chapter it tells of the king of Assyria, Sennacherib, nearly has control of Jerusalem in Judah (The Southern Kingdom), but has not entered the city and speaks to all the people of Judah that there God is no better than any other God, that his fathers have beaten and conquered, as well as himself. It is written in my Bible as such:

And the Lord sent an <u>angel</u>, which cut off all the mighty men of valour, and the leaders and captains in the camp of the king of Assyria. So he returned with shame of face to his own land. And when he was come into the house of his god, that they came forth of his own bowels slew him there with the sword.

So the Lord saved Israel and the King of Israel.

Now there are two things I want you to think on and one being what type of angel this would be? To me he had a lot of work to do in a short period of time, so I am going with a destroyer angel, but I also think it could be a captain of a group of angels, but more than a messenger. How about a captain of the Cherubim's? Why do I think like this, read this next question?

Near the end of this verse it states that "they came forth from his own bowls and slew him with a sword". Was he depressed and killed himself and everyone just said it was their God that did it; or did angels come out of him and then slew him with a sword once he was with his god, to show his god he is nothing? Or were they demons? Or could it have been his own people for he failed to win this war and came back empty handed and no troops?

Sometimes the Bible leaves us wondering why, what, how, when. But it is for us to discover, which means more studying. I know there is literature on this king of Assyria and some time I will look it all up and decide from there. For now I like the idea that he committed suicide for he had nothing left. But I will let you decide and maybe some scholar will let us know.

___

The Book of Ezra
The theme of this book is: Restoring the temple.
This book ends where Second Chronicles leaves off. With the encouragement from the prophets, Haggi and Zechariah, the temple was rebuilt. Ezra led the exiles back home only to find the others had fallen back into sin. Ezra then preached God's words and the people repented.

EZRA—There are no angels in this book that I can remember. If I am wrong, please forgive me and let me know, thank you.

The Book of Nehemiah

The theme of this book is: The wall rebuilt and people restored.

This book is about Nehemiah who was sent by a Persian king with a third wave of exiles to Jerusalem to rebuild the cities walls. Nehemiah had opposition from the people who had moved into the land, but with God in his heart and with joy of the Lord as his strength, he overcame. Nehemiah also served as governor, twice.

NEHEMIAH 9:6—In this chapter it is telling about all the tribes of Israel were fasting and praying, and reading the law from the Book of Moses, which reading took one fourth of the day, and one fourth they confessed their sins, and their forefather's sins, and worshipped the Lord. In their praying to the Lord, it was mentioned that: (As it is worded in my Bible)

Thou, even thou, art Lord alone; thou hast made heaven, the heaven of heavens, with all their host, (angels) *the earth, and all things that are therein, the seas, and all that is therein, and thou preservest* (preserve, protect) *them all; and the host of heaven* (angels) *worshippeth* (worship) *thee.*

Sometimes things look wrong in their spelling, but it is in the old English language and is what is in the Bible. In this verse it just mentions "hosts of heaven", so to me it is talking about "all" the angels in heaven.

The Book of Esther
The theme of this book is: God provides and protects.
This book is about Ester who was living among the exiles in Persia and who became the Queen of Israel. She was prepared by God "for a time like this", when Haman, a Persian official tried to get rid of the Jewish minority. This book documents of the origin of the observance of Purim, the celebration of Israel's survival and God's faithfulness.

There are no angels in this book, but go ahead read it and prove me wrong. Thanks.

_____
_____
_____

The Book of Job
The theme of this book is: God is sovereign.
This book of Job is a dialog of why God allows good people to suffer. The book contains to Job's faith and God's vindication of Job's trust in him. Genuine faith cannot be destroyed. This book is regarded as a theological and literary masterpiece.

JOB 4:15-21—In this verse it talks of a spirit, not an angel, but I do believe good spirits could be slightly higher than an angel, and I believe this one to be a good spirit. Why a good spirit, Job does not lose anything else, as it was Satan that took everything from him. As you read this think of someone talking to you. Remember Job lost everything, but did not leave God and when God saw all this; he gave Job more than what he originally had. This is how it is worded: (I will put slash marks in between sentences so it may be easier to understand) If unable to understand this, ask your pastor or get on line and use your computer and type in Definition of

Job 4:15-21. (Also the New International Bible has a good definition.) Think of it this way, the spirit is referring to God.

Then a <u>spirit</u> passed before my face; the hair of my flesh stood up: / It stood still, but I could not discern the form thereof: / an image was before mine eyes, there was silence and I hear a voice saying, / Shall mortal man be more just than God? / Shall a man be more pure than his maker? / Behold he put no trust in his servants; and his <u>angels</u> he charged with folly: / How much less in them that dwell in houses of clay, whose foundation is in the dust, which are crushed before the moth? / They are destroyed from morning to evening: they perish for ever without regarding it. / Doth not their Excellency which is in them go away? They die, even without wisdom.

This will continue on through chapter five and Job will be told that he will have many children again, and everything will come back to him. (Money, animals etc…) Even though Job is starting to question everything happening to him, he still has his faith in God, so Satan looses another battle. We will now go to Chapter 38.

JOB 38:7—In Verse 7, God is talking to Job and asking him where he was when he (God) made everything. Now this just mentions angels and I want you to think what it says and then I will give you the answer. It reads as such:

<u>When the morning stars sang together, and all the "sons" of God shout for Joy?</u>

Now I want you to take your time and read this chapter and figure out everything God is telling or asking Job. It is an interesting conversation. Also take some time and read two chapters before and two chapters after this chapter. I do believe it is interesting reading.

Now did you see what the angel's were??? It just says the <u>Sons of God</u> shout for joy; and that means all the angels in heaven. Now it also says, "When the morning stars sang together", and did you know that it took centuries to find out that all the stars have a tone, or a radio wave sent out through the heavens, so they "sing together". There are a lot of other scientific items throughout the Bible and if I remember correctly, it is around one hundred; and I do mention a few of them in one of my other books titled "Does Your Flame Flicker? Remember the <u>Son of God</u> is Jesus; the <u>sons of God</u> are angels. One letter makes a big difference.

Quote:—When hearts listen, Angels sing.
Sunday school joke. (Author Unknown)
At Sunday school they were teaching how God created everything, including human beings. Little Johnny, a child in the kindergarten class, seemed especially intent when they told him how Eve was created from one of Adams ribs. Later in the week, his mother noticed him lying on the floor, as though he were ill, and asked Johnny what was wrong. Johnny replied; I have a pain in my ribs, so I guess I am getting a wife. His mother said "WHAT? Getting a WIFE"? So Johnny told her what the Sunday school teacher had told him and his mother laughed for hours over little Johnny, getting a wife.

CHAPTER FIVE

GOOD ANGELS OF THE OLD TESTAMENT
BOOKS OF PSALMS, PROVERBS, ECCLESIASTES, SONG OF SOLOMON, ISAIAH, JEREMIAH, LAMENTATIONS, EZEKIEL, DANIEL

The Book of Psalms
The theme of this book is: God is worthy of worship.

This book is filled with songs and prayers with many of them being written by King David. Some pertain to the treasures of wisdom, God's word, and the troubled heart of mourners, while others praise God with song and invite others to sing praises to the Lord.

PSALM 8:5—This is a Psalm of David, and is a very short Psalm containing only nine verses. This is where an angel is only mentioned, and it pertains to glorifying the Lord. You should read this entire Psalm, (and it will only take you a minute) to understand the meaning of this Psalm. Now this is how verse five is worded:

For thou hast made him (man) *a little lower than the angels, and hast crowned him in glory and honor.*

It says what it says, we are a little lower than the angels, but we still have glory and honor.

PSALM 33:6—Another psalm of David, and again it just mentions angels, and this is how it is worded:

By the word of the Lord were the heavens made; and all the HOST of them by the breath of his mouth.

Now this one mentions the Host of them, which covers all the angels. You should read all the Psalms for it will give you more information when you study your Bible and sometimes it is just a refresher course, or it will cover an item that you skipped over and did not fully understand. It will help you in studying your Bible.

PSALM 34:7—Just another Psalm of David that only mentions angels. This is how it reads in my King James Version Bible:

The angel of the Lord encampeth (Stays near) *about them that fear him, and delivereth* (Helps) *them.*

Remember that fear is "respect or awe" for the Lord, so if you love the Lord, the angels will take care of you in your troubled times. (You still, must have faith).

PSALM 35:5, 6—One more Psalm of David's and it just mentions angels as well. In this psalm he is just asking God to not only protect him from those that wish to harm him, but also those that are after his soul. This is how this verse is worded:

Let them be chaff (Loose seed coverings) *before the wind: and let the angel of the Lord chase them. Let their way be dark and slippery; and let the angel of the Lord persecute* (Oppress, harass) *them.*

(At the end of this Psalm, David is again glorifying the Lord.)

PSALM 68:17—This is listed as a Psalm or a Song of David's, and pertains to the Lord's enemies being scattered and those that hate him flee before him. This is how verse 17 reads:

The chariots of God are twenty thousand, even thousands of angels: the Lord is among them, as in Sinai, in the holy place.

I do hope you noticed it says there are thousands of angels, but also mentions that God is among them.

PSALM 78:49—This Psalm is called a Maschil (or Maskil) of "Asaph". Maschil can mean a few different things, such as; understanding, meditation, poem, skillful, wise, or a composed song, or to teach. Now different scholars will say it is this, and so on, but to me it means to teach. Again, when you are reading, please read all of the Psalms and study them as you read. Do not forget to look things up or ask questions from others that are well versed in the Bible. Now I want you to pay close attention to this one, and this is how it is worded that mentions angels:

He cast upon them the fierceness of his anger, wrath, and indignation, and trouble, by sending "evil" angels among them.

This I believe is one of the first instances that God is using evil angels. Why, you ask? For all the good that God has done for the People of the Israel nation, they still sinned and did not believe, and some still worshipped idols. So the people would pay for their mistakes until God said that's enough. Then the people would behave themselves for awhile, but then would start all over again. They just never seemed to learn from their past mistakes, and as "some" of our youth today would say—Man, they don't get it.

PSALM 91:11-12—This Psalm is actually a prayer of Moses, the man of God. Again just read the complete Psalm to understand it better. Again this Psalm just mentions angels.

For he shall give his angels charge over thee (you), to keep thee in all thy ways. They shall bear thee up in their hands, lest thou dash thy foot against a stone.

When you do read this Psalm, please read all of Psalm 90 as well or you may get a little lost. This Psalm is just telling you to believe in God and he will have angels watch over you. I hope also that you noticed that this is the Psalm that I used in the front of this book.

PSALM 103:20—This is another Psalm of David and only mentions angels, but in a slightly different manner, for David is blessing the Lord for all that the Lord has done for David, and the people of Israel. This is how my Bible is worded: (Remember I use the KJV Bible) also read the complete Psalm.

Bless the Lord, ye (you) *his <u>angels</u>, that excel in strength, that do his commandments, harkening unto the voice of the Lord. Bless ye the Lord, all ye his <u>hosts</u>, ye ministers of his, that do his pleasure.*

In this small verse he mentions both angels and hosts, and I and some scholars think that both of them pertain only to angels.

PSALM 104:4—This Palm goes along with Psalms 105, 106, and 107. Here David is thanking the Lord for all our blessings, from when he made the earth and the heavens, to all he has done for us, including things he has allowed us to make with our own hands. This is the part where the angels are mentioned:

Who maketh (makes) *his <u>angels</u> spirits, his ministers a flaming fire.*

Now as you read does it really mean he made his angels spirits to drink? "No", I do not think so, and what I want you to do is look up the word spirit and see just what you find out. There are a lot of meanings and yes, there is a definition of alcoholic beverages with this. But I think it will mean "all" the others before you get to alcoholic beverages. I suppose some scholar will say no, it pertains to spirits that you drink, but I do not see it that way and I think I am right, so there.

PSALM 148:2-5—Actually this is one Psalm of six that "Praise" the Lord written by David. (See Psalms 145 through 150) So, if you wish to praise the Lord these Psalms are what you are looking for. The verse that mentions angels is worded as such in my King James Version Bible:

Praise ye him, all his <u>angels</u>; praise ye him, all his <u>hosts</u>. Praise ye him, sun and moon, praise ye him, all ye stars of light. Praise him, ye heavens of heavens, and "ye waters that be (are) above the heavens". Let them praise the name of the Lord, for he commanded, and they were created.

I know, the way it is worded there are angels and hosts, but all the literature I have read, says they both are angles. If you find something different, please let me know. The only definition in a dictionary, which I like for a host, is a large group of people or things. So I am sticking to all the angels together. Thanks.

Did you see that I put (") around seven words. I wanted to get your attention and hopefully I did. I read somewhere years ago that in the days of old, they believed the water came from heaven when it rained, as most thought heaven was just above the clouds. Whoever wrote the article then claimed that the people believed like it is written, that the water was just above the clouds, in heaven. I probably will never find that article again as it was a very long time ago, and it is plausible. Now some articles I have found on angels, you would need three degrees from schools of higher learning to understand the articles and there is just very little data to go by. (Scholars, please help the ordinary people out, write items so we can understand them.) This is all of the angels that I found in the Books of Psalms.

The Book of Proverbs
The theme of this book is: Wisdom and righteousness. This book is about wisdom for living, with the wicked stumbling in the darkness, while a path of the righteous is like the light of dawn glowing brighter all day. This book is written by different authors.

PROVERBS—In this book there are no angels that I can remember, but I want you to read this book anyway. If you find any angels in the book let me know so I can change my notes. Thanks. The main reason I want you to read this book is because it has a lot to do with life, and what you should do to help others, such as the poor. Now I want you to think on this, and yes I believe YOU CAN do it. You can be an ANGEL here on earth, by helping out at shelters for the homeless, the out of work person, hungry children, abused children, children who are orphaned, the elderly, maybe your neighbor. They may not say a word about their problems, but just go talk to them (even buy them a cup of coffee) just so they talk and get it out of their system. Buy them food or groceries, etc: JUST BE AN ANGEL, TODAY.

The Book of Ecclesiastes
The theme of this book is: Contentment and joy.
This is one of those books I believe should be taught a lot more, as you will see as you read this. This is a reflection

of a preacher (Old Man) as he questions the meaning of life. We all chase after the good things of life with some things satisfying us for a time, but death will end our satisfaction. People, especially the young, should believe in God while they have the rest of their lives before them, so they can enjoy God's gifts.

ECCLESIASTES 5:6—This book in the bible was written by Solomon and is a book of joy and contentment, with a lot of words that deal with vanity, Solomon's vanity. This is how it is worded:

Suffer not thy mouth to cause thy flesh to sin; neither say thou before the <u>angel</u>, that it was in error; wherefore should God be angry at thy voice, and destroy the work of thy hands.

This is the only passage that I know of that speaks of an angel, and I suppose I could be wrong, but I do not think so. As I have said in the past, it is better to read SLOWLY and STUDY what you read, and it will be easier for you to learn. After you have read the whole Bible, I recommend you read it again as you will be surprised at what you missed the first time. Do you understand this passage from the Bible?? Did you do something wrong and say it was not you, for your angel will know, and then God will know and what you have worked for, will be gone. Does that sound like this passage? That is the way I look at it, but others may look at it a different way.

This Book is the Song of Solomon
<u>The Theme of this book is: Love songs.</u>
This book is the accumulation of love poems between man and woman, celebrating the sexual loyalty God intended for marriage. God established marriage, including the real union

of man and woman. The love between a husband and wife fashions a bond that is "strong as death". This book celebrates such inspiring love.

SONG OF SOLOMON:—This was written by Solomon and is considered a love song, and I see no indications of angels in this song, or poem (as some say it is). I would like you all to read this book slowly, and I want you to decide what you think it really is for. Now Solomon was a lover and he had three hundred wives and seven hundred concubines, and no one really knows yet how many children he really had. Then he went against the Lord by marrying foreign wives, which God told him not to do and the first foreign wife was a Pharaoh's daughter from Egypt. According to other literature, he had a love affair with the Queen of Sheba who was Ethiopian and it is said that she gave birth to a boy, who ruled the land of Ethiopia and was a believer in the Jewish faith, and practiced it daily. I sometimes believe he wrote this for her, but other scholars say it is to God, and others say, other people, like his many wives or concubines. Woops—I am getting off the subject of angels, sorry about that, it is something though that I would like you to read and decide who you think, that he wrote it too. It is a great piece of literature, or poem, or song, but just take your time and look things up if you are confused by what it says.

The Book of Isaiah
The theme of this book is: Judgment and comfort.
This book is about Isaiah the prophet who lived during the decline of Israel, and spoke the word of God to people who were "deaf and blind" to God. The people refused to listen to

Isaiah, and he warned them of their sins and also taught that God is the highest. Isaiah tells of Cyrus the Persian who would lead the people out of exile and also that someone would be wounded for our trespasses, which would accomplish God's purpose of salvation. This book also tells of a new world were God would rule as King, judging the evil ones, and giving eternal peace.

ISAIAH 6:2—This Book of the Bible tells of Isaiah talking to the people of Israel that are left, which this is their judgment but also he tries to comfort them. He is telling them that in the year that King Uzziah died he saw the Lord sitting upon a throne; (and it is written as such in my Bible); and he talks of seeing these angels:

Above it stood the <u>seraphim's:</u> each one had six wings; with twain (Two) he covered his face, and with twain (Two) he covered his feet, and with twain (Two) he did fly. And one cried unto another, and said, Holy, Holy, Holy, is the Lord of hosts; the whole earth is full of his glory. And the posts of the door moved at the voice of him that cried, and the house was filled with smoke. Then said I, Woe is me! For I am undone; because I am a man of unclean lips, and I dwell in the midst of a people of unclean lips: for mine eyes have seen the King, the Lord of hosts. Then flew one of the <u>seraphim's</u> unto me, having a live coal in his hand, which he had taken with the tongs of the altar; and he laid it upon my mouth, and said, **Lo, this hath touched your lips; and thine iniquity is taken away. And thy sins purged.**

I do hope you noticed what types of angels were there. Did you notice how many wings and what they were for? How did they purge Isaiah's mouth and lips for saying unclean things? If you do not remember, go back and re-read this paragraph.

Okay; I know someone is still lost, so the angels are SERAPHIM'S and they have SIX WINGS, They were used to cover their feet, face and to fly. They put a hot coal on Isaiah's lips, from the altar of God to purge Isaiah's lips, for they were unclean.

I want you to very slowly read this book of the Bible, Isaiah, and it will tell of the Lord going to punish the people of Israel more, by making the land barren without cities. Then God changes his mind and gives the Israeli people a reprieve. Our Lord has done this for the Israeli people over and over, and they still do not learn.—If you do not read slowly you may get lost very fast in this book of the Bible.

ISAIAH 37:36—This is where the Lord is talking and saying that the King of Assyria will not get close to the city (Jerusalem) and will never shoot an arrow at the city. For the Lord will defend the city for his own sake and for the sake of David, his servant. It then switches to an angel and this is how it is worded in my Bible:

Then the angel of the Lord went forth, and smote (struck) *in the camp of the Assyrians a hundred and four score and five thousand; and when they arose early in the morning, behold, they were all dead corpses.*

Then when the king of Assyria left Israel and went home, his sons killed him with the sword and one of his sons then ruled the land of Assyria. Now for what this angel does, I believe there is only one answer to what type of angel he would be; a destroyer angel of the Lord's.

ISAIAH 63:9—I want you to read a couple of chapters before this verse to understand this part of the book. It deals with the salvation of Jerusalem. Now sometimes as I read this it sounds like Isaiah is getting some things off his chest, but I could be wrong on that, so I am going to let you decide for yourself. The verse that mentions an angel is worded as such:

In all their affliction he was afflicted, and the angel of his presence, saved them; in his love and pity he redeemed them, and he bare (took care of) *them, and carried them all the days of old.*

As I keep reading this chapter and verse, I do believe this angel to be more than a messenger angel, more like a captain of a group of angels, do you agree? Again the Bible leaves you to decide for yourself, the Bible makes you think, which is what you have to do when you do anything in your life, think.

Guess what happens next; the people of Israel rebelled, and vexed (Irritated) his Holy Spirit. Then the Lord was not happy with them again. Just think; this has been going on since Moses started leading the people out of Egypt, and they still do not understand what God wants from them. They would rather worship idols and sin, and no one really understands why. Then God would do something against them and they would straighten up again, for awhile.

The Book of Jeremiah
The theme of this book is: Judgment of Juda.

This book is about Jeremiah (or weeping prophet) who had a message of God's judgment. He dictated his predictions to Baruch, a scribe and told the people of the coming of God's judgment. God's instructions to him were "to pluck up and break down" and also to "build and plant". Jeremiah sees a day when God will write his law on human hearts, saying they shall all know Him and He will remember their sin no more.

There are no angels listed in this book, but just check, for I could have goofed and missed one.

The Book of Lamentations
The theme of this book is: Mourning for Jeruslem.
This is a book of five poems telling of the grief over the fall of Jerusalem. It is like a eulogy at a funeral, but here, it is the fall of a nation. It was written to produce hope in God whose mercy is now with them every morning.
Once again, this is another book with no angels.

The Book of Ezekiel
The theme of this book is: Judah's judgment and restoration.
This book is about Ezekiel, who was a prophet and a priest and was one of those exiled to Babylon. He ministered for (approximately) twenty three years. Ezekiel was aware of God's presence in our lives and preached to those left in Judah and to the exiles with messages of warning and judgment, telling of the fall of Jerusalem. His vision of dry bones in a valley is one example of God's ability to breathe new life into those who are spiritually dead.
EZEKIEL 1:4-26—As you read this book about Ezekiel, read it slowly and imagine what Ezekiel thought and said; and remember that Ezekiel was a prophet and was in captivity along with all the Israeli people, including King Jeholachin. At the start of this chapter he mentions that the heavens opened up and he saw visions of God; this is the start of verse four as it is in my Bible. (This one is rather long, but worth reading.)

And I looked, and behold, a whirlwind came out of the north, a great cloud, and fire infolding (Folding inside) *itself, and the brightness was about it, and out of the midst thereof as the colour of amber, out of the midst of the fire. Also out of the midst thereof came the likeness of four living creatures. And this was their appearance; they had the likeness of a man, and every one had four faces, and every one had four wings, and their feet were straight feet, and the sole of feet like the sole of a calf's foot; and they sparkled like the colour of burnished brass. And they had hands of a man under their wings on the four sides, and they four had their faces and their wings. Their wings were joined one to another; they turned not when they went; and they went every one straight forward. As for the likeness of their faces, they four had the face of a man, and the face of a lion, on the right side; and they four had the face of an ox on the left side; they four had the face of an eagle. Thus were their faces; and their wings were stretched upward; two wings of every one were joined one to another, and two covered their bodies. And they went straight forward; whither the spirit was to go, they went; and they turned not when they went. As for the likeness of the living creatures, their appearance was like burning coals of fire, and like the appearance of lamps; it went up and down among the living creatures; and the fire was bright, and out of the fire went forth lightning. And the living creatures ran and returned as the appearance of a flash of lightning. Now as I beheld the living creatures, behold one wheel upon the earth by the living creatures, with his four faces. The appearance of the wheels and their work was like unto the colour of beryl* (blue or green stone): *and they four had one likeness, and their appearance and their work was as it were a wheel in the middle of a wheel. When they went, they went upon their four sides, and they* *turned not when they went. As for their rings, they were so high that they were dreadful; and their rings were full of eyes round about them four. And when the living creatures went, the wheels went by them; and when the living creatures were lifted up from the earth, the wheels were lifted up. Whithersoever the spirit to go, they went, thither was their spirit to go, and the wheels were lifted up over against them; for the spirit of the living creature was in the wheels. When those went; these went; and when those stood, they stood; and when those were lifted up from the earth, the wheels were lifted up over against them; for the spirit of the living was in the wheels. And the likeness of the firmament upon the heads of the living creatures was as the colour of the terrible crystal, stretched forth over their heads above. And under the firmament were the wings straight, the one towards the other; and every one had two, which covered on this side, and every one had two, which covered on that side, their bodies. And when they went, I heard the noise of their wings, like the noise of great waters, as the voice of the Almighty, the voice of speech, as the noise of an <u>host</u>; and when they stood, they let down their wings. And above the firmament that was over their heads was a likeness of a throne, as the appearance of a sapphire stone; and upon the likeness of the throne was a likeness as the appearance of a man above upon it.*

Then the Lord starts talking to Ezekiel and tells him what to say to the people of Israel, for he was not happy with them. I do hope you take your time reading all of Ezekiel, or you may get very lost.

Now did you notice that these angels had four wings, not six like we talked about earlier, and these had four faces as well.

Now as I read all of this, I can see why some people think it is about UFO'S, and if you do not read EVERYTHING before and after what is here, you will be going to bed tonight thinking; "Holy cow, there are aliens that came to earth". But would God be with them? And would they be in a vision? Or could aliens be in Heaven? Some people will think that Ezekiel was on a bad drug trip, and the way it is worded, who knows. When we get to heaven let's hope we find out what is what; and I do not think I would like seeing these angels as then I might think I was doing drugs. No thank you. I do think I would want to run the other way though; I'm not a coward, just cautious.

Then after the Lord is through speaking with Ezekiel it mentions the following, which is Chapter 3, Verses 12 and 14. Think about this as you read and try to understand what is written.

Then the spirit took me up, and I heard behind me a voice of great rushing, saying, blessed be the glory of the Lord from this place. I heard also the noise of the wings of the living creatures that touched one another, and the noise of the wheel over against them, and a noise of great rushing. So the spirit lifted me up, and took me away, and I went in bitterness, in the heat of my spirit; but the hand of the Lord was strong upon me.

I once heard a scholar say that a spirit "is" God, or his only son Jesus Christ. Then I read that depending on how it is used, it can also mean a messenger of God and can even mean an evil spirit or unclean spirit. So please read slowly so you understand "everything", and if you do not understand it all then it is time to ask a pastor or a good group Bible teacher. As you read all the way up to chapter ten, you will find spirit mentioned again and again. To me these are all good spirits, unless it says they are not and I consider them all messengers of God.

Also you will find a man dressed in a white linen robe, with an inkhorn on his side. When you read this, is it talking about an angel, or a man? If you said angel you are correct. What is the angel doing with an inkhorn and a ruler? He is measuring the New Jerusalem and the temple in heaven that will be on earth, some day. I hope that is what you thought of as well.

EZEKIEL 10:1-22—Now this chapter does have a lot of angels in the wording, so please read slowly and try to understand what you are reading; some of this is like reading it a second time as it was in earlier descriptions, in an earlier part of the chapter.

Then I looked and behold, in the firmament (or earth, separating the waters above in heaven and the water beneath the earth) *that was above the head of the <u>cherubim's</u> there appeared over them as it were a sapphire stone, as the appearance of the likeness of a throne. And it spake* (spoke) *unto the <u>man cloaked with linen</u>, and said,* **<u>Go in between the wheels, even under the cherub, and fill thine hand with coals of fire from the cherubim's, and scatter them over the city.</u>**

(Now to me as I read this, it "is" God talking to the man dressed in white linen—an angel.)

And he went in my sight. Now the <u>cherubim's</u> stood on the right side of the house, when the <u>man</u> went in; and the cloud filled the inner court. Then the glory of the Lord went up from the <u>cherub</u>, and stood over the threshold of the house; and the house was filled with the cloud, and the court was full of the brightness of the Lord's glory. And the sound of the <u>cherub's</u> wings was heard even to the outer court, as the voice of the Almighty God when he speaketh (speaks)*. And when it came to pass, that he had commanded the <u>man clothed with linen</u>,* saying; **Take fire from between the wheels, from between the cherubim's;** then he went in, and stood beside the wheels. And one <u>cherubim</u> stretched forth his hand from between the <u>cherubim's</u> unto the fire that was between the <u>cherubim's</u>, and took thereof, and put it into the hands of <u>him that was clothed in linen</u>; who took it and went out. And there appeared in the <u>cherubim's</u> the form of a man's hand under their wings. And when I looked, behold the four wheels by the cherubim's, one wheel by the <u>cherub</u>, and another wheel by another <u>cherub</u>; and the appearance of the wheels was the colour of a beryl (Blue or green stone) stone. And for their appearances, they four had one likeness, as if a wheel had been in the midst of a wheel. When they went upon their four sides; they turned not as they went, but to the place whither (wherever) the head looked they followed it; and turned not as they went. And their whole body, and their backs, and their hands, and their wings, were full of eyes round about, even the wheels that all four had. As for the wheels, it was cried unto them in my hearing, O Wheel. And every one had four faces; the first face of a cherub, and the second face of a man, and the third face of a lion, and the fourth face of an eagle. This is the living creature that I saw by the river in Chebar (A Canal in Mesopotamia). And when the <u>cherubim's</u> went the wheel went by them; and when the cherubim's lifted up their wings to mount up from the earth, the same wheels also turned from beside them. When they stood, these stood, and when they lifted up, these lifted up themselves also; for the <u>spirit</u> of the living creature was in them. Then the glory of the Lord departed from the threshold of the house, and stood over the <u>cherubim's</u>. And the <u>cherubim's</u> lifted up their wings, and mounted up from the earth in my sight; and when they went out, the wheels also were beside them, and every one stood at the door at the east *gate of the Lord's house; and the glory of God of Israel was over them above. This is the living creature I saw under the God of Israel by the river of Chebar; and I knew they were the <u>cherubim's</u>. Every one had four faces apiece, and every one had four wings; and the likeness of the hands of a man under his wings. And the likeness of their faces was the same faces which I saw by the river Chebar, their appearances and themselves; they went every one straight forward.*

Then it goes back to what Ezekiel is to do with the people of Israel, manly prophesying to the people that the Lord is unhappy with them, and what the Lord will do to them. As I said a little earlier, Ezekiel saw all this in a dream; and I know I have had dreams (which could be classified-nightmares) after I have eaten something that did not agree with me and have also taken medicine prescribed by my doctor that made me dream weirdly. So sometimes I wonder what he ate or smoked, or whatever before he had his dream, or was it actually angels and the Lord in this dream? And some people think this is just something to do with UFO'S. Sure it could sound like it is from outer space, and I suppose to some that is what it is. But no, this is a dream and only our Lord would let you dream like this. And NO, do not go there, it is not about UFO'S, it's about angels and angels only. One other thing I thought about, why is his angels so much different than other angels? I believe Ezekiel was just (as our children would say) freaked out by all this as it would have been new to him. Think about how you would react, and could you tell this story the same way over and over? Sometimes I have trouble remembering what I dreamed about, how about you???

EZEKIEL 40:3 THROUGH ???—No, I did not make a mistake, there is a lot of reading for you to do and can start at chapter forty, verse three, and read most of the rest of the book of Ezekiel. Now a lot of scholars say this does not pertain to an angel while others and I do. (Although I am not a scholar) Most of this is God talking to Ezekiel and when you get to verse three, this is the way it is worded:

And he (God) b*rought me thither, and behold, there was a <u>man</u>, whose appearance was like the appearance of brass, with a line of flax in his hand, and a measuring reed* (A measuring rod from a water plant, usually six cubits in length)*; and he stood in the gate. And the <u>man</u> said unto me,* **Son of man, behold, with thine eyes, and hear with thine ears, and set thine heart upon all that I show thee; for in the intent that I show them unto the art thou brought hither** (here)**; declare all that thou seest to the house of Israel.**

Now most of this chapter deals with a man measuring the temple, but it is an angle of the Lord. Then it goes back to God talking to Ezekiel. What type of angel is a good question; and it does not really say what type of an angel it would be. I would believe that it is an angel that is high up in the command of angels to be entrusted with the measuring of the temple in heaven to be brought to earth and to be built in Jerusalem.

Later in the book of Ezekiel, Chapter forty six, I believe, it tells of a prince shall enter by the way of the porch of that gate. My question to you is, could this be the first indication of Jesus' coming to Jerusalem? Really think on that question that I just asked, and then reread the entire chapter. Read it real slow and you decide for yourself or ask your pastor or a Bible group study leader, to explain this—If he can. Remember the Bible can be confusing, especially if you read too fast, so please take your time. Myself I do believe it could be Jesus coming to Jerusalem. I know some scholar will say "OH, NO" it can't mean that, it means this.—I know I got off the subject of angels, sorry, but I just had to put it in.

The Book of Daniel
The theme of this book is: End time prophecies.

This book tells about Daniel who was exiled to Babylon and was chosen to serve in the court of Nebuchadnezzar. When the Persians conquered Babylon he was given a position of power, but still remained faithful to God. From his ability to interpret dreams, and also the story of the fiery furnace, the lion's den, the handwriting on the wall, and the apocalyptic visions, with all of it leading to god's sovereignty over human concerns.

DANIEL 3:25—This is when Nebuchadnezzar the king told everyone to worship a golden calf and three people did not, so he put them in a fiery furnace. These three were Shadrach, Meshach, and Abednego, and when the king saw four men walking around the fiery furnace he was startled, and his people all said that only three men were put in the fiery furnace. This is how it is worded in my KJV Bible:

He answered and said Lo, I see four men loose, walking in the midst of the Fire, and they have no hurt; and the form of the fourth is like the Son of God.

Yes, it does say like the form of the SON OF GOD, but no, it is not Jesus, and most scholars say it is just an angel, as Jesus was not even thought of as yet among humans on earth. I do believe he could be a little higher than a messenger and would go with a captain of one of the groups of angels. (We will just have to wait and see what type of angel it was when we go up to heaven ourselves, so we can find out.)

DANIEL 3:28—Continuing on, it is worded as such in my Bible:

Then Nebuchadnezzar spake (spoke) *and said, Blessed be the God of Shadrach, Meshach, and Abednego, who hath sent his <u>angel</u>, and delivered his servants that trusted him, and have changed the kings word, and yielded their bodies, that they might not serve nor worship any god, except their own God.*

The king then goes on to praise God and even says he will cut the people into pieces if any one says anything bad against God and that their houses would be made into a dunghill. (A pile of animal excrement) So the king changed his mind rather quickly after seeing how the fire did not harm any of the three or the angel. Now this story has been told thousands of times in Sunday schools all over the world, and also has been sung in Sunday school and in churches many, many, times.

DANIEL 4:13-17—This is a dream that King Nebuchadnezzar had and no one could give him a definition of the dream, until he called in Daniel. Now, Nebuchadnezzar's god had given a name to Daniel which was Belteshazzar. This is how it is worded in my Bible:

I saw in the visions of my head upon my bed, and behold, a <u>watcher</u> and an <u>holy one</u> came down from heaven; he cried aloud, and said thus; Hew (cut) *down the tree and cut off his branches, shake off his leaves, and scatter his fruit; let the beasts get away from under it, and the fowls from his branches: Nevertheless leave the stump of his roots in the earth, even with a band of iron and brass, in the tender grass of the field, and let it be wet with dew of heaven, and let his portion be with the beasts in the grass of the earth: let his heart be changed from man's, and let a beast's heart be given unto him; and let seven times pass over him. This matter is by the decree of the <u>watchers</u>, and the demand by the word of the <u>holy ones</u>; to the intent that the living may know that the most High ruleth in* *the kingdom of men, and giveth it to whomsoever he will, and setteth up over it the basest* (lowest, poorest) *of men.*

Then Daniel, after a long consideration of the dream, gave this explanation to Nebuchadnezzar as written in my Bible:

My lord, the dream be to them that hate thee, and the interpretation thereof to thine enemies. (We will skip down to verse 25) *That they shall drive thee from men, and thy dwelling shall be with the beasts of the field; and they shall make thee to eat grass as oxen, and they shall wet thee with the dew of heavens,* (every morning you will be wet from the morning dew) *and seven times shall pass over thee, till thou know that the most high ruleth in the kingdom of men, and giveth it to whomsoever he will. And they command to leave the stump of the tree roots; thy kingdom shall be sure unto thee, after that thou shall have known that the heavens do rule. Wherefore, O king, let my counsel be acceptable to thee, and break off thy sins by righteousness, and thine iniquities* (immorality) *by showing mercy to the poor; if it may be a lengthening of the tranquility* (quiet, peacefulness).

I know it is hard to understand, as it is written in the old English, but read it slowly, look words up, and then decide what it all means. Even though Daniel tried warning King Nebuchadnezzar, he did not follow what the watchers and the holy ones were telling him, through Daniel. And all that was in the dream befelled him. (Came true) I hope you realize that the watchers in this dream of Daniels seem to be good angels, along with the holy ones. Now if you did not understand the above vision interpretation by Daniel, think of it as such; the king's enemies will tear down his kingdom and he will be forced to live outside with the beasts that live in the field and the king would be wet from the morning dew for he had no protection. If he did not change his ways and stop sinning, and should also help the poor then he does not understand that God is the one who is in command of all men, not the king, and all of what Daniel has told him will happen—and it did.

DANIEL 6:22—This section of the chapter pertains to Daniel while the Israelites were in captivity. The king of the Chaldeans gave Daniel a position above princesses and governors of the kingdom for Daniel was well liked by the king. The princesses and governors tried to get Daniel out of the way and came up with a plan, that all would sign a deal with the king, that all would have to go through the king and that no man could go through a god or idol without first going through the king. And if they did they would be thrown in into a lion's den. So they watched for Daniel to pray to his God, and then told the king, and Daniel was thrown into the lion's den. The king had to obey this decree but did not wish to, and he slept not and arose early and rushed to the lion's den. This is how it is worded in my KJV Bible:

Then the king arose very early in the morning and went in haste unto the den of lion's. And when he came to the den, he cried with a lamentable (crying out in grief) *voice unto Daniel; and the king spake and said to Daniel, O Daniel, servant of the living God, is thy God, whom thou serest* (Pray to) *continually, able to deliver you from the lions? Then said Daniel unto the king, O king, live for ever: My God hath sent his <u>angel</u>, and hath shut the lion's mouths, that they have not hurt me; forasmuch as before him innocency was found in me; and also before thee, O king, have I done no hurt.*

The king was glad that no harm had come to Daniel; but brought those who accused Daniel and threw them, their wives and children into the lion's den, and they were no more.

It does not say much about the angel, but it could be a messenger angel, but I do lead toward an angel higher up like a captain of a group of angels. I will let you make your own decision, unless a scholar can come up with a better one.

DANIEL 7:10—This is during the time Daniel was having a dream, and the fourth beast came forth and he was told about the death of the beast and what it meant. The part on angels is worded as such:

A fiery stream issued and came forth from before him; <u>thousand thousands ministered</u> unto him; and <u>ten thousand times ten thousand stood before him</u>; the judgment was set, and the books were opened.

This only mentions all the angels standing and ministering to God, and if you read verse nine it will tell you a little about God, but nothing about what his face actually looks like.

DANIEL 7:16—Daniel is grieved by the visions he is having and is troubled by them; my Bible words it like this: *I came near unto one of them that stood by, and asked him the truth of all this. So he told me, and made me know the interpretations of the things.*

Now I know this is not easy to understand especially if you are a fast reader, so slow down and absorb what you are reading, and do not forget to look things up or ask your pastor for help. (I have a hunch some pastor will not be happy with me, for they may not know themselves.) Next read all of chapter seven and it goes on between Daniel and the angel. Now this could be the angel telling Daniel what is what. But when I read it, it sounds like Daniel is also telling the angel. "Another spot in the Bible that may confuse a lot of people", but I believe it is the angel telling Daniel all that needs to be known. I also believe this angel to be just a messenger angel.

DANIEL 8:13-27—In this section to me it is just a vision of Daniel's and tells of the Host Of Heaven, but does not really talk about angels, or what they do. This section can also be confusing if read too fast so slow down, and try to understand what is written. (It may be worthwhile to read a couple of verses before and after this verse.) Is it the Host of Heaven or not? That is my question to you. Now in this section it also tells of "Gabriel", but the way it is mentioned I want you to try to decide if it is the archangel, Gabriel. To me it is, but the way it is written it does make it a little confusing, that is why you have to read slowly and absorb everything you read.

Okay, just keep reading the next verses and I think you will really make up your mind about it being the archangel, Gabriel.

DANIEL 9:21-27—This verse picks up from Chapter 8, verse 21 and tells of Gabriel talking to Daniel; Now I did not list each verse and I will skip a verse here or there, not to confuse you, but to help you and if you have a lot of nothing to read it "may" confuse you. That is why I skipped them.

Yea, while I was speaking in prayer, even the man <u>Gabriel</u>, whom I had seen in the vision at the beginning, being caused to fly swiftly touched me about the time of the evening oblation (Offering). *And he informed me, and talked with me, and said* ***O Daniel, I am now come forth to give thee skill and understanding. At the applications the commandments came forth, and I am come to shew thee; for thou art greatly beloved; therefore understand the matter, and consider the vision.***

This just means that Daniel is to consider the vision he had, and that Gabriel will show him what to understand all that was in the vision.

(We jump to verse 24) ***Seventy weeks are determined upon thy people and upon the holy city, to finish the transgression, and to make an end of sins, and to make reconciliation for*** *iniquity, and bring in everlasting righteousness, and to seal up the vision and prophecy, and to anoint the most Holy.*

The people have seventy weeks to stop sinning and end their transgressions, then they will have everlasting righteousness, and to anoint the most holy of people.

Know therefore and understand, that from the going forth of the commandments to restore and to build Jerusalem unto the Messiah the Prince shall be seven weeks, and threescore and two weeks: The street shall be built again, and the wall, even in troubled times.

The people have seven weeks, and threescore (60x7) and two weeks to restore Jerusalem and the streets and the wall, even in troubled times.

And after threescore and two weeks shall Messiah be cut off, but not for himself: and the people of the prince that shall come and destroy the city and the sanctuary; and the end therefore shall be a flood, and unto the end of the war desolations are determined. To me Gabriel is saying, if not finished in that time, that a prince from elsewhere will come and destroy everything, including the sanctuary and the city, and then there will be a flood, and like the end of a war there will be desolation.

And he shall confirm the covenant with many for one week; and in the mist of the week he shall cause the sacrifice and the oblation (offerings, or gifts) *to cease, and for the overspreading of abominations* (horrible, or disliked) *he shall make it desolate, even until the consummation,* (ending) *and that determined* (firm feelings) *shall be poured upon the desolate* (lonely).

God will allow a lot of people to come to him for a half a week, then God will cause the sacrificing and the oblation to cease, and will make it desolate for the people.

Now remember this is Gabriel talking to Daniel, describing what will happen if the people of Israel do not heed or hear God's words and to follow his laws. I do hope you remember who Gabriel is, if not go to the front of the book and look him up.

DANIEL 10:5-10—All of the book of Daniel is like a big vision to him, but he has these dreams and he is the one to interpret these dreams, for the Lord makes sure he understands them. This section is about the time when Cyrus, the king of Persia, controlled the Israeli people.

Now I want you the reader to read from the beginning of Chapter 10; this is where Daniel is beside a river called Hiddekel, (Tigris River) and then read all the way through to the end of the Chapter. Read it slowly and let it soak in, as a lot of this is an angel talking to Daniel, and no it is not God talking to him.

The angel is clothed in linen, whose loins (area below waist) were girded (surrounded) with fine gold of Uphaz. (A place known for its gold, where, unknown) The body also was like the beryl, (mineral used in gemstones) and his face as the appearance of lightning, and his eyes as lamps of fire, and his arms and feet like in color to polished brass, and the voice of his words like the multitude. (Many voices) Now as I read, there are others with Daniel, but he is the only one to see and hear, while the others hid their faces.

Now it sounds to me that the angel that was sent was having problems with another king and Michael, one of the chief princes came to help that angel so he could come to Daniel. Nowhere do I see it was God himself. As I Said, just read it slowly and go over it many times if you are having trouble understanding, and look words up if you are having trouble; then if you still are lost, talk with your pastor. (I know if I saw an angel similar to this one, I might run the other way; I prefer the perfect ones depicted in pictures.)

The Book of Hosea
The Theme of this book is: God's love for Israel.
This book is about Hosea, the death bed prophet, who prophesized before the fall to Assyria. His ministry followed a golden age in the northern area, with peace and prosperity since Solomon. But the prosperity led to moral decay and the people started worshipping idols. So God had Hosea marry a prostitute, whose unfaithfulness served as a example of Israel's unfaithfulness to God. He then told the people of their punishment to come unless they returned to God and was faithful to God.

HOSEA:—This is a small book of the Bible, and I found no angels listed along with the following list of other books of the Bible (Old Testament) that have no angels either. Now I am getting old but I am not blind as a bat, maybe ugly like a bat (Who said that?) to some people's eyes. That is why I always get into trouble; I say things at the wrong time. But just check all the books and see if I am right or wrong, then let me know. (Please)

Here is a list of other books of the Old Testament without angels listed:

Joel—with the theme of this book being: The days of the Lord

This book is about the prophet Joel, but very little is known about him. He seems to have ministered in Judah, telling of a locust plaque (which did strike Israel). He also gave the people a hint about the "day of the Lord". The Israeli people believed that God would restore Israel to its former glory. According to Joel, God would not only punish other nations, but Israel itself for they were being unfaithful. He told the people to repent, as God would "pore out his spirit on all flesh", in the coming days of Pentecost.

Amos—With the theme of this book being: Judgment of Israel.

This book is about Amos who was believed to be the first prophet (or nearly first) to write. He was a farmer and a shepherd called to prophecy during the reign of Uzziah, who reigned in the southern part of the kingdom (Judah) with Jeroboam II reigning in the northern part of the kingdom (Israel) with both kingdoms having stability, but this was leading to idolatry and corruption. Amos denounced the people and warned them that disaster would fall upon them for breaking the covenant. Amos urged the people to leave their dishonesty and instead to "let justice roll down like waters". He also told that God would remember his covenant with Israel and would restore the covenant with the people.

Obadiah—With the Theme of this book being: Edom's doom.

This book is the shortest book of the Old Testament, written after the armies of Babylon destroyed Jerusalem. The people of Edom would capture the fleeing Israelites and turn them over to the Babylonians, This angered God as the people were related to the Israelites and should have been helping them. Obadiah told that Edom would be repaid for mistreating God's people and in or about one hundred years, Edom was in ruin. Obadiah also prophesied that God's love for his people would revive the House of Jacob.

Jonah—With the theme of this book being: Mission to Gentiles.

Some scholars have said this book is a book of fiction for it contains a story of a fish swallowing a man. In Second Kings, it mentions that Jonah was living during the reign of Jeroboam II and Jesus considered him a factual person in the book of Matthew. The book of Jonah focuses on the prophet himself instead of a message. When God sent Jonah to Nineveh, he rebelled and was swallowed by a fish, then after repenting, God returned him to land and he went on to preach in Nineveh. The reason Jonah rebelled was made clear after Nineveh repented, for Jonah speculated that God would forgive the people of Nineveh and was angered by this.

Micah—With the theme of this book being: Restoration of Judah.

This book tells of Micah a prophet in Judah during the reign of Jothm, Ahaz, and Hezekiah, approximately the same time as Isaiah. During the time of prosperity, Micah denounced the wealthy, who oppressed the poor, and warned of bad things to come. The Northern Kingdom did fall and the Southern Kingdom almost fell. This book has three sections, switching between warnings and words of hope. Micah talked of peace among all nations, when all people could "beat swords into plowshares", and that someone would bring forth the people of Israel and would be born in Bethlehem.

Nahum—With the theme of this book being: Judgment of Nineveh.

This book tells of a century after Nineveh repented and was spared, they would no longer repent and Nahum preached on this and a few years later Nineveh fell to Babylon. His prophecies were directed at the people of Judah, who will rejoice at the fall of Nineveh.

Habakkuk—With the theme of this book being: Live by faith.

This book was written before the fall of Assyria. God had used Assyria to punish Israel and then Babylon to punish Judah. This one prophesy, was fulfilled years after Habakkuk, who had questioned how can God use a wicked nation, like Babylon, for this purpose. Habakkuk then says that God judges all nations and Babylon would be judged some day, even though God's ways are mysterious at times, the "righteous shall live by faith while waiting salvation.

Zephaniah—With the theme of this book being: The day of the Lord.

This book is about when Zephaniah who was a prophet and during the time of King Josiah who was the one that brought spiritual revival to the Kingdom of Judah right after the reign of King Manasseh, which was disastrous. Zephaniah preached of God's judgment and of the people's corruption and wickedness. He also preached his plan to restore Judah, and spoke of the "Day of the Lord," when sin would be punished and justice would prevail, with some of the faithful being saved. No detail is given for the "Day of the Lord," but speaks of the consequences and calls the people to work for the Lord.

Haggi—With the theme of this book being: Rebuilding the temple.

This book is about the first wave of exiles that returned from Babylon to Jerusalem and started rebuilding the temple, but they gave up. After being motivated by Haggi and Zechariah, they finally completed the rebuilding of the temple. Haggi had ridiculed the people living in paneled houses while the temple lay in ruin. He called them to repent and renew their covenant with God as the temple was a symbol of God's presence; and love returned to his people.

Hey, that is a few books that you do not have to study, does that make you happy???

Well, You ARE Wrong. I want you to read all of them anyway; otherwise you will never read the Bible on your own. (Well, a few of you will not).

And did you realize that that there are only two more books in the Old Testament and one of those does not have angels listed either; and that is <u>Malachi</u>, so that only leaves you with one to go and then we will start on the New Testament. Here is the last one for you to study, and if you want, go brew a cup of coffee, or tea, or whatever; then start to read.

The Book of Zechariah

<u>With the theme of this book being: Preparation for the Messiah.</u>

This book tells of Zechariah who inspired the people to repent and renew their covenant with God. It would be necessary for the people to be ready to worship God once the temple was finished. He reassured the people of God's comfort and care, and then hope was restored with the ordination of Joshua as priest and Zerubbabel as governor. The book ends with God's promise that he would rule over all the earth.

ZECHARIAH: 1:9-20—For your information, scholars have taken the Book of Zechariah and have divided it into two sections, calling the lower section; (Through chapter eleven) Deutero-Zechariah and the rest; Trito-Zechariah. (Through chapter fourteen). This is what I am working on trying to figure out why, and someday I hope to have it completed, and when I do, I will let you know. If you find it first let me know, please.

Now these are all visions that Zechariah had, and it is wise to read right from verse one through verse seven before going farther. It tells of Zechariah receiving the word from the Lord of Hosts, but does not really say if it is an angel or if is God himself. I myself would go with an angel and as you read I would think you would do the same. When you get to verse nine it does mention an angel, and goes like this in my Bible, from verse eight on:

I saw by night, and behold a <u>man riding a red horse</u>, *and stood among the myrtle* (Evergreen tree with fruit and flowers-Mediterranean area) *trees that were in the bottom; and behind him were there red horses, speckled and white. Then said I, O Lord, what are these? And the* <u>angel</u> *that talked with me said unto me,* **I will show thee what these be.** *And the* <u>man</u> *that stood among the myrtle trees answered and said,* **These are they that the Lord has sent to walk to and fro through the earth.** (Verse 11) *And they answered* <u>the angel</u> *of the Lord that stood among the Myrtle trees, and said,* **We have walked to and fro through the earth, and behold, all the earth sitteth still, and is at rest.** *Then the* <u>angel</u> *of the Lord answered and said,* **O Lord of hosts, how long wilt thou have mercy on Jerusalem and on the cities of Judah, against which thou had indignation these threescore and ten years.** (Verse 13) *And the Lord answered the* <u>angel</u> *that talked with me with good words and comfortable words. So the* <u>angel</u> *that communed* (Talked) *with me said unto me,* **Cry thou, saying. Thus saith the Lord of hosts: I am jealous for Jerusalem and for Zion with a great jealousy.** (Verse 15) **And I am very displeased with the heathen that are at ease: for I was a little displeased, and they helped forward the affliction. Therefore thus saith the Lord; I am returned to Jerusalem with mercies: my house shall be built in it, saith the Lord of hosts, and a line** *shall be stretched forth upon Jerusalem. Cry yet, saying, Thus saith the Lord of hosts; My cities through prosperity shall be spread abroad and the Lord shall yet comfort Zion, and shall yet choose Jerusalem.*

(Verse 18) *Then lifted I up mine eyes, and saw, and behold four horns. And I said unto the <u>angel</u> that talked with me; What be these? And he answered me.* **These are the horns which have scatterd Judah, Israel, and Jerusalem.**

(Verse20) *And the Lord showed me four carpenters. Then said I, What come these to do? And he spake saying.* **These are the horns which have scattered Judah, so that no man did lift up his head: but these are come to fray** (Fight) **them, to cast out the horns of the Gentiles, which lifted up their horns over the land of Judah to scatter it.**

Now this angel I believe is just a messenger angel, for all he does is talk to Zechariah.

ZECHARIAH 2:1—Before I get into Chapter two, I want you to think about something. In the verse above it talks of four carpenters, and they would fight the Gentiles and to cast out the horns that were over Jerusalem and Judah. Where else do you find mention of a carpenter? Was it not Joseph that married Mary when she was pregnant with Jesus? And did not Jesus also learn the carpentry business when he was young? Sometimes things like this just grab me when I read and study the bible and I like to try and put two and two together. Here God is using carpenters in the Old Testament and again in the New Testament. Hopefully you understand what I am talking about. God uses us in more than one way, has he used you? Or where you not paying attention to what he was telling you? Sorry I am getting away from angels again, but the Bible does things to me when I read and try to teach others. Okay back to angels.

(Chapter two)—You will need to read this complete chapter to understand what is going on. I will try to put it in my words so you get an idea of what is what. Now Zechariah saw a man with a measuring line in his hand, who was going to measure Jerusalem from width to length, "without walls", for the multitude of men and cattle therein. These are all angels that are in this Chapter, including the man with the measuring line. Then the angel said to Zechariah:

For I, saith the Lord. Will be unto her a wall of fire round about, and will be the glory in the midst of her.

Then it goes on farther and mentions that God will bring the people back to Jerusalem and he will be amongst them in the city. Again I do believe this angel is just a messenger angel, but the one with the measuring line could be a little higher up, like a captain of one of the groups of angels.

ZECHARIAH 3:2—Angels are the only thing mentioned in this Chapter along with Joshua (That is right, Joshua), and with the Lord doing the talking, and Satan is looking on. One verse has an angel talking as such:

(VERSE 6)—*And the angel of the Lord protested unto Joshua saying:* **Thus saith the Lord of Hosts; If thou will walk in my ways, and if thou keep my charge, then thou shalt also judge my house and shalt also keep my courts, and I will give you thee places to walk among these that stand by.**

Now as you continue reading this chapter, you see it is sort of confusing, as where does the angel stop talking and where does the Lord start talking? Some scholars believe it is all angel and others believe it is both the Lord and the angel and is just giving the information to Joshua. Now as you read verse eight, you will find the word "BRANCH". The definition of this word as used here in Zechariah is: "The person would function as both king and priest, and would rebuild the temple of the Lord when Jerusalem was restored". I do hope you understand, as that is the simplest way I can put it.

ZECHARIAH 4:1—Actually you could read this complete book as it is nearly all about angels talking to Zechariah and what he saw. It will be hard to follow, but I know you can do it, just remember to read it very slowly. It also tells of God's instructions to Zechariah, but just remember the following as you read:

Zechariah has eight night visions (or dreams) with the Chapters one through six which are:

1—The Horesmen—chapter 1:7

2—The Horns and the craftsmen (Carpenters)—chapter 1:18

3—The man (angel) and the measuring line (ruler)—chapters 2:1

4—Joshua, the high priest and Satan—chapter 3:1

5—The Lampstand (seven lamps) and the olive trees—chapter 4:1

6—The flying scroll—chapter 5:1

7—The woman in the basket—chapter 5:5

8—The four chariots—chapter 6:1

In chapters seven through eight the Lord has four messages for Zechariah and the people of Israel, which are:

1—Rebuke—Other countries will no longer live in Jerusalem.

2—Remind—The Lord tells us what to do, but we do not listen, and do not hear the widowed, the orphan, the fatherless, and think of ourselves only.

3—Restoration—Jerusalem will be restored.

4—Return—the people will return to Jerusalem and the Lord will live there as well.

The two burdens of Zechariah, chapters nine through fourteen.
1—Burden against other nations.
2—Burden for Israel.

The one thing, when you read all of this (that I believe), that it is telling of the Messiah coming to Israel. To me anyway, it is telling that some day that the Messiah will come, even down to the thirty pieces of silver. Now as you read this entire book of the Bible you also find the carpenters, and Joseph was a carpenter and he also taught Jesus how to work with his hands. And throughout the Bible there are references to Jesus in the Old Testament, but are covered up and hard to find, you just have to think and study as you read. Even though it is in the Bible the Israeli people did not learn, and still today they do not consider Jesus the Messiah (Unless they are a Christian Jew). Well no matter what I think, somebody out there will say I am wrong and may even say I am a false teacher. But as I write this I know that the Lord has been with me while I write, and God <u>has</u> corrected me one way or another as I write (Even crashing my computer so I had to start all over with this book and I changed a few items).

Well, you got through the Old Testament and the good angels, and now we go to the New Testament and start with the good angels throughout these books. Hope you are ready, if not take a break and come back later, (but not too much later) or you may forget what you have already learned.

Well, you forgot already, one more book to read and that is listed below.

_____
_____
_____

The Book of Malachi
Malachi—The theme of this book is: Call to repentance. (No angels listed that I remember anyway, but old age is stepping in here and there, so read it and prove me wrong.)

This book is when the call to repent has gone unheeded and God has not restored the covenant blessings, so Malachi writing a short time later, called the people to repent, as the priesthood was corrupt, worship was just routine, divorce was everywhere, and tithing was disregarded. The Lord asked through Malachi, "Will man rob God," but promised to "open the windows of Heaven" to those who pay their full tithe. Malachi predicted the "messengers of God" were coming. (This was John the Baptist, along with our Lord, Jesus Christ.)

Well, if you are not cheating and have been reading the Bible, you are through with the Old Testament. NOW—let's go on to the New Testament.

Quote: I believe in angels from heaven, and on earth, I am surrounded by them, and some I know by name, and I call them friends. Do you have a friend you can call an angel?

Dear God prayer; It rained for our whole vacation and is my father mad! He said some things about you that people are not supposed to say, but I hope you will not hurt him anyway. Your friend—(But I am not going to tell you my name)

—

Dear God,
In Sunday school they told us what you do. Who does it when you go on vacation??—Jane

—

Dear God,
Are you really invisible, or is it a trick?—Lucy

CHAPTER SIX

THE NEW TESTAMENT
GOOD ANGELS OF THE BIBLE
BOOKS OF MATTHEW, MARK, LUKE, JOHN, ACTS, ROMANS

The Book of Matthew
The theme of this book is: Coming of the king.
This book tells of that Jesus is Israel's Messiah, also telling of Jesus healings and casting out of Demons. It then teaches of the "Sermon on the Mount", the "Parables of the Kingdom", and the "Olivet Discourse". Also you will find the "beatitudes" and the "Lord's Prayer". Matthew also writes about the conflict between Jesus and the religious leaders, finishing with Jesus' statement of "Seven Woes" upon them. This book centers on Jesus' ministry and his death and resurrection.

MATTHEW:—As you noticed (I hope) that I did not put down a chapter or verse, and there is madness in my thinking: Well maybe.

I want you to read in chapter one, an interesting piece, that not to many people think about at all. And in all the years of going to church, I do not remember anybody preaching about this. It is short but I do believe that it is a part of the Israeli history. Then after that we will get back to angels; I promise.

Chapter one, verse seventeen:—*So all the generations from Abraham to David are fourteen generations; and from David until the carrying away into Babylon are fourteen generations; and from the carrying away into Babylon unto Christ are fourteen generations.* (A generation is usually forty years, from birth to birth; so 40 x 14 equals 560 years; times three equals 1560 years total time span).

Most of the Bible uses the number seven and occasionally, twelve, and this little piece, as small as it is, is very significant in the Israeli history. Was God telling us something here? That is a question for you to think on and see if anybody can come up with a good answer. Does your pastor know? When you think on this a little bit, it really is the number seven doubled, and number seven is used very heavily throughout the whole Bible. (This author does think it means more than we realize it does, and why would God use such a number so often?)

This is the Bible, deep, guiding, mysterious, intriguing, history, love, laws, suspense, and yes, murder. Now, we will go back to angels.

MATTHEW 1:20:—This is when Joseph is considering what to do with Mary, for she is pregnant and it is not his.

But while he thought on these things, behold, the angel of the Lord appeared unto him in a dream, saying. **Joseph, thou son of David, fear not to take unto thee Mary thy wife; for that which is conceived in her is of the Holy Ghost.** *(God's)*

And she shall bring forth a son, and thou shalt call his name JESUS: for he shall save his people from their sins.

Jesus will save the people only from "their SINS", it does not say anything else, but he did a lot more, like healing people etc; I do hope you are following this, it is simply put but you do have to think a little, God did so in the Old Testament, and Jesus does it in the New Testament. Think people, Think.

MATTHEW 1:24:—This is how it is worded in my Bible:

Then Joseph being raised from sleep did as the <u>angel</u> of the Lord had bidden (told) *him, and took unto him his wife.* (Mary)

MATTHEW 2:13:—This is when Joseph takes the family to Egypt to flee Herod. (After Jesus is born)

And when they departed, behold, the <u>angel</u> of the Lord appeareth to Joseph in a dream, saying, **Arise, and take the young child and his mother, and flee to Egypt, and be thou there until I bring thee word; for Herod will seek the young man to destroy him.**

Herod was very angry, for the wise men left the country without telling him where the child was, and decided to kill all the children under his reign from the age of two and under.

MATTHEW 2:19:—This is after Herod's death.

But when Herod was dead, behold, an <u>angel</u> of the Lord appeareth in a dream to Joseph in Egypt. Saying: **Arise, and take the young child and his mother, and go into the land of Israel; for they are dead which sought the young child's life.**

Now all this was told before the time of Joseph and came true, by the profit Jeremy. (Jeremy is a synonym (different word) for Jeremiah) If you look his name up, you may not find Jeremy, only Jeremiah.

MATTHEW 4:11—This is just after Jesus was tempted by Satan, right after he baptized John and John baptized Jesus.

Then the devil leaveth him, and behold, <u>angels</u> came and ministered unto him.

We will cover more of this when we go through the Bible covering Satan. Just read all of Matthew and learn more about Jesus and his ministry, and take your time and absorb all of it into thine (your) head. Woops, must be the old English is catching up to me.

MATTHEW 13:39 then 41-42 then 49—This is during the time when Jesus is preaching parables and his disciples ask him to teach them the parable of the field. This is some of what Jesus said to them, you really have to read it very slowly to comprehend it.

The enemy that sowed (plant) *them is the devil; and the harvest is the end of the world; and the reapers are his <u>angels</u>.*

The verse above should not really be in here, but can you figure out why? Really read it close, what is it all about? Is it not talking about the devil and these are HIS angels, not God's. (The reapers are the Devils angels) This is why I keep harping about taking your time reading and understand what you are reading, looking things up on the internet or in other books. Then if you are confused just ask your pastor or a Bible study teacher. If you read this too fast you would think that God's angels would reap the harvest. One small sentence can really be confusing.

The son of man shall send forth his <u>angels</u>, and they shall gather out of his kingdom all things that offend, and them which do iniquity (wickedness)*: And shall cast out into a furnace of fire; there shall be wailing and gnashing of teeth.* (They will go to Hell)

So shall it be at the end of the world; the <u>angels</u> shall come forth, and sever (Separate) *the wicked from among the just.*

As I said just a minute ago, please read all of what Jesus has to say, but very slowly so you can figure out what he is talking about. Now all this was said just before John the Baptist lost his head after the girlfriend of Herod asked for John's head, and he did so, just to satisfy a woman that was not his.

MATTHEW 16:27—This is right after Peter trying to rebuke Jesus, and Jesus tells him: Get behind me Satan. It is worded as such:

For the Son of man shall come in the glory of his Father with his <u>angels</u>; and then he shall reward every man according to his works.

Jesus will come to earth again in GLORY of his Father and will bring all the angels with him.

I hope you realize that all the angels in Matthew after chapter thirteen are just mentioned. Without the type of angel or what they really will do, not even a hint of any message, given by them from God.

MATTHEW 18:10—This is worded as such, just after Jesus calls to a little child and sets him in the midst of the disciples:

Take heed that ye despise not one of these little ones; for I say unto you. That in heaven their <u>angels</u> do always behold the face of my father which is in heaven.

I hope you understood what it is saying; Do not harm a child that believes, for his angel will give a bad report about YOU to our Father in Heaven.

MATTHEW 22:30—This is how it is worded in my KJV Bible: It relates to the Sadducees asking Jesus a question of who will be married to whom if a wife looses a few husbands and then they all are in heaven, does she go with the first or the last husband. Jesus answered as such;

For in the resurrection they neither marry, not are given in marriage, but are as the <u>angels</u> of God in heaven.

Jesus goes on from there and you should read all of it to understand what he says. The last thing he says (which I like the best) is;

God is not the God of the dead, but of the living.

MATTHEW 24:31—This is when Jesus was on the Mount of Olives, and is asked by the apostils, what the sign would be for his return to earth and the end of the world. Read the entire chapter to understand what is being said. This is part of Jesus answer;

And he shall send his angels with a great sound of the trumpet, and they shall gather together his elect from the four winds, from one end of heaven to another.

Now Jesus does say from the four winds, from one end to another—BUT it says "heaven" not earth, once gathered, they will come to earth, but when God says to. A lot of people, as I have said before, read too fast and see things that are not there.

It then goes on to say:

But on that day and hour knoweth no man, no, not the angels in heaven, but my Father only.

Nobody at any time will know the time that it will be, for the end of the world, only God will know. So all the predictions that you hear of about the end of the world YOU can just toss in the waste basket. When it is time it will be the time and only God will know when that will be.

<u>MATTHEW 25:31</u>—This is right after Jesus tells the parable of three men given money by their master, with one trading and gaining the same amount of money back, likewise the second man did the same, but the last man buried his coin and when his master came home he had only the coin to give his master. Therefore his master took the coin and gave it to the man that had five coins and gave back ten coins, leaving the third man with nothing. This is right after that:

When the Son of man shall come in his glory, and all the holy <u>angels</u> with him, then shall he sit upon the throne of his glory.

I want you to read the rest slowly and really think on what it says until you get too Chapter 26. I believe you have all heard this in church sometime, if not just take your time reading and if confused ask you pastor or a Bible class instructor. (I keep telling people to ask their pastor, in my other books as well, and I wonder if they do not like me yet; or if I am considered a friend). Pastors, remember your ten commandments when you think of me, I am just trying to teach your flock that you should be teaching.

MATTHEW 26:53—The apostle Judas has just kissed Jesus and the soldiers have taken hold of Jesus, with one of the disciples taking his sword and cutting off an ear of a servant of the high priest. Then Jesus said:

Put up again thy sword into his place; for all they that take the sword shall perish with the sword. Thinkest thou that I cannot now pray to my father, and he shall presently give me more than twelve legions of <u>angels</u>? But how then shall the scriptures be fulfilled, that thus it must be?

What he is saying here, is that the scriptures (along with the profits); say that the apostles not do anything, for Jesus knows that he will be put to death, for it is written. And anyone that kills by the sword will die by the sword. Jesus also mentions that if he wished, he could bring twelve legions of angels to his aid, if needed

MATTHEW 28:1-7—I will put all of verse one through verse seven here, but I want you to read all of this chapter, for it is important for you to learn what Jesus did after he was risen and what happened with Mary Magdalene and the disciples.

In the end of the Sabbath, as it began to dawn toward the first day of the week, came Mary Magdalene and the other Mary to see the sepulcher. And behold, there was a great earthquake for the <u>angle</u> of the Lord descended from heaven, and came and rolled back the stone from the door, and sat upon it. His countenance was like lightning, and his raiment white as snow. And for fear of him the keepers did shake, and *became as dead men. And the <u>angel</u> answered and said unto the women,* **Fear not ye: for I know that ye seek Jesus, which was crucified. He is not here: for he is risen, as he said. Come, see the place where the Lord lay. And go quickly, and tell his disciples that he is risen from the dead: and, behold, he goeth before you into Galilee; there shall ye see him: lo, I have told you.**

The only thing that I have found is the angel is a male for it refers to HIS throughout these verses. And since he was sort of assigned to roll back the stone and to tell everyone that Jesus has risen, I would think he would be a higher rank and would be like a captain of a group of angels.

NOTE: I want you to look at the last word of the Book of Matthew, what is it? There are how many books in the Bible that ends in this word? I am not giving you the answer; I want you to look them all up so you can understand your Bible better. That word is one we use all the time and is the word— ***AMEN.***

Quote: A Christ centered life is like a good watch, open face, busy hands, pure gold, and full of good works.

—

Dear God jokes.

—

Dear God,
Is it true my father won't get in heaven if he uses his bowling words in the house?—Anita

—

Dear God,

I went to a wedding and they kissed right in church. Is that okay?—Neil

Dear God,
Thank you for the baby brother, but what I wanted was a puppy.—Joyce

_____
_____
_____
_____
_____
_____

Book of Mark
The theme of this book is: Jesus the servant.

This book is the second gospel and was written by Mark, explaining that Jesus is the Christ, also that Jesus declared the Kingdom of God, healed the sick, and died for all our sins. Mark shows that there are three groups of people with none of them understanding Jesus, The religious leaders had Jesus arrested, his disciples left him, and the crowds mocked him. Then after Jesus died on the cross it took a Roman centurion to realize that Jesus <u>was</u> the Son of God.

MARK 1-13—As you start to read Mark it will talk of the Spirit like a dove descending on Jesus. This is a good Spirit, but then you read that the Spirit driveth (Drives) him into the wilderness. Then at the end of Jesus being in the wilderness it ends and is worded as such:

And he was there in the wilderness forty days, tempted by Satan; and was with the wild beasts; and the <u>angels</u> ministered unto him.

Angels and the Angel of Light 117

The angels tend to Jesus "after" Satan temps him, and then it goes on to talk of John the Baptist being put in prison.

It does not say what type of angel and only that they tend to Jesus, so I look at it that they would not be just a messenger but higher up in the ranks. I know someone will say that they are just messengers, but that is okay, I do not mind.

MARK 8:38—This is when Jesus is talking to the people and asks them who will come after me, let them deny himself, and take up his cross and follow me. Then it goes on to say:

Whosoever therefore shall be ashamed of me and of my words in this adulteress and sinful generation; of him also shall the Son of man be ashamed, when he cometh in the glory of his Father with the holy <u>angels.</u>

In other words, do not be sinful, believe in Jesus, and when he returns he will remember you, otherwise you will only know that hot place that has all that fire raging in the pit. (Called Hell)

MARK 12:24 & 25—This is when one of the apostles asks Jesus a question about a woman who takes a husband but has no children and then he dies and his brother takes her as a wife and has no children, and this is repeated for seven brothers, all having no children and all dying. Then she dies and they want to know what husband she should be with in heaven? And Jesus replies:

Do ye not therefore err, because ye do not know the scriptures, neither the power of God? For when they shall rise from the dead, they neither marry or are given in marriage, but are as the <u>angels</u> which art in heaven. Now the only problem I do see with this statement by Jesus is, that some scholars say that we do not become angels in heaven, and when you read this you can say that this says you do, but it states; "but are as" the angels in heaven. So does it really mean you will be in heaven as the angels are, but you are not a real angel? I am going to let the scholars decide on that one, but to me it means we will be in heaven only.

MARK 13:32—Again this is when the apostles ask Jesus what the signs are when the time will be the second coming. This is near the end of Jesus' answer:

But of that day and that hour knoweth no man, no, not the <u>angels</u> which are in heaven, neither the Son, but the Father.

Only God knows when the time of Jesus return will be, and Jesus does not even know. My question to you today is: Are YOU ready for when Jesus returns to earth? Just do not answer: I want you to think for awhile, like overnight, and then answer it truthfully. Thanks.

MARK 16:4-7—This is slightly different than Matthew, but very little. In Mark it does not say an angel but is worded to sound as if it were an angel. It reads as such in my Bible:

And when they looked, they saw that the stone was rolled away; for it was very great. And entering the sepulcher, they saw a young man sitting on the right side, clothed in a long white garment; and they were affrightened. (Frightened) *And he saith unto them, be not affrightened: Ye seek Jesus of Nazareth, which was crucified: he is risen; he is not here; behold the place where they laid him. But go your way, tell his disciples and Peter that he goeth* (goes) *before you into Galilee, there shall ye see him, as he said unto you.*

There are two items in this chapter that I want you to think on and maybe ask your Pastor or Bible class teacher to teach us what, why, where, etc:.

Did you notice in the last verse it says "tell his disciples and Peter"? Why was Peter singled out? I know my answer is simple but you best ask your Pastor to make sure I am right.

My answer is that Peter is the most loved of all the disciples; do you think that is right?

At the beginning of this chapter it tells of three people coming to the sepulcher (burial place), and they are Mary Magdalene, Mary, the mother of James, and Salome. Where have you heard the name Salome before? Can you remember? Think hard and think of John the Baptist. Thankfully this Salome is not the same one that received John the Baptist's head. This Salome is a follower of Jesus and who ministered to him in Galilee and traveled with him to Jerusalem. Mary may be (scholars have not much proof of this) the mother of James and John.

So you see how easy it can be to get confused and why you have to look things up. I wonder how many people over all these years have thought that this is the one that received John's head, and now she is at the tomb of Jesus bringing spices for the burial of Jesus. You have to study as you read, and understand what you read, or you can be wrong later down the road.

_____
_____
_____

Here is a small story to break up the boring studying of this book on angels.

The First Stone: Jesus saw a crowd chasing down a woman to stone her and approached them. "What is going on here, anyway?" he asked. One of the crowd responded, "The woman was found committing adultery and the law says we should stone her!"

Wait Jesus yelled, "Let he who is without sin cast the first stone." Suddenly, a stone was thrown out from the sky, and knocked the woman on the side of her head.

"Aw, c'mon Dad..." Jesus cried. "I'm trying to make a point here."

_____
_____
_____
_____
_____
_____

Book of Luke

The theme of this book is: Christ's humanity and compassion.

This book is the third Gospel and written by Luke as a letter to Theophilus. He wrote this after reviewing the facts about Jesus and then he documented the birth of Jesus, going through Jesus' ministry, death and resurrection. Jesus carried out his ministry using the power of the Holy Spirit, preaching the good news of salvation; also telling of Jesus' sympathy for the poor and the lonely. Jesus fulfilled prophesy and his purpose was to search for and save the lost. This Gospel tells of the parables the "Good Samaritan" and the "Prodigal Son".

LUKE 1: 11-38—Yes that is right, twenty seven verses, to read, but everyone should know most of this as it is when the angel appeared to Mary to tell her she is pregnant with the Lords Son, Jesus Christ. It also is the story of Elizabeth becoming pregnant with John (John, The Baptist). So I am only going to mention the angel's part and let you read all of it. It is very simple reading so you all should do okay as long as you think while you read. Now Zacharias did not really believe the angel Gabriel, so Gabriel caused Zacharias to not be able to speak until John was born. Here are the different verses that mention an angel:

Verse 11—*And there appeared to unto him* (Zacharias) *an angel of the Lord standing on the right side of the alter of incense.*

Verse 12—*And when Zacharias saw him (angel), he was troubled, and fear fell upon him.*

Verse 13—*But the angel said unto him,* **Fear not, Zacharias; for thy prayer has been heard; and thy wife Elizabeth shall bear thee a son, and thou shalt call his name John.**

Verse 18—*And Zacharias said unto the angel, Whereby shall I know this? For I am an old man, and my wife well stricken in years.*

Verse 19—*And the angel answering said unto him,* **I am Gabriel, that stand in the presence of God; and am sent to speak unto thee, and to shew thee these glad tidings.**

Verse 26—*And in the sixth month the angel Gabriel was sent from God unto the city of Galilee, named Nazareth.*

Verse 28—*And the angel came unto her* (Mary), *and said,* **Hail, thou art highly favoured, the Lord is with thee; blessed art thou among women.**

Verse 30—*And the angel said unto her,* **Fear not, Mary, for thou hast found favor with God.**

Verse 34—*Then said Mary unto the angel, How shall this be, seeing I know not a man.*

Verse 35—*And the angel answered and said unto her.* **The Holy Ghost shall come upon thee, and the power of the Highest shall overshadow thee: therefore also that holy thing which shall be born of thee shall be called the Son of God.**

<u>Verse 38</u>—*And Mary said, Behold the handmaid of the Lord; be it unto me according to thy word. And the <u>angel</u> departed from her.*

I should not even think of putting this down, but there could be someone out there that still does not know what type of angel this is: This is more than a messenger angel, for he is one of the top angels in heaven, and archangel named Gabriel.

<u>LUKE 2:9</u>—This is during the time Joseph and Mary, who was carrying Jesus, were going to Bethlehem for it is the time to be taxed and people go back to where you were from, and he was in the family of David so that is where they went. While they were there, Mary gave birth to Jesus and it is in my Bible as such: (It starts with the angel talking to the shepherd's).

<u>Verse 9)</u>—*And, lo, the <u>angel</u> of the Lord came upon them, and the glory of the Lord shone round about them; and they were sore afraid.*

<u>Verse 10)</u>—*And the <u>angel</u> said unto them,* **Fear not; for, behold, I bring good tidings of great joy, which shall be to all people.**

<u>Verse 13)</u>—*And suddenly there was with the <u>angel</u> a multitude of the <u>heavenly host</u> praising God, and saying.* <u>Verse 15)</u>—*And it came to pass, as the <u>angels</u> were gone away from them into heaven, the shepherds said one to another. Let us go even unto Bethlehem, and see this thing which is come to pass, which the Lord hath made known unto us.*

All these angels I do believe to be just messenger angels. Someday I do want to go through all of the gospels and see what is different in each one, do they add more to the story or take away from the story, and who is who different in each of the four books. Just to compare each one and then decide who the best writer of the four was.

Angels and the Angel of Light 123

LUKE 12:8-9—This is when Jesus was talking to an innumerable multitude of people (and the scribes and Pharisees urge Jesus to say many things to see if they can destroy him by catching him saying something he should not). In my Bible its states this; as Jesus is starting to talk to his disciples and the people:

Verse 8)—*Also I say unto you, Whosoever shall confess you before men, him shall the Son of man also confess before the <u>angels</u> of God.*

Verse 9)—*But he that denieth me before men shall be denied before the <u>angels</u> of God.*

These angels are only talked about by Jesus to tell the disciples that the people that say he is NOT the Son of God, the angels will say so before God. Those that are with Jesus, they also, will be said so before God, but in a good way. I want you to read this entire chapter to get the right perspective of it. We will go on with Luke.

LUKE 15:10—This is when Jesus is talking again to a crowd with the Pharisees and scribes murmuring about Jesus sitting with sinners and eating with them.

Likewise, I say unto you, there is joy in the presence of the <u>angels</u> of the God over one sinner that repenteth. I hope you understand what is written here, all it is saying is, as long as you repent your sins and do not do them again, the angels of God in heaven, will rejoice.

LUKE 16:22—Now this is when Jesus is still talking to a crowd, along with the disciples and the Pharisees tried to ridicule Jesus but he tells them they live to keep men happy, not God, which is wrong. So Jesus told this story of the beggar and the rich man, where the beggar was trying to get crumbs from the rich man's table and all he got was his sores licked by the rich man's dogs, after the dogs ate the crumbs; And the beggar died.; Verse 22 is the only mention of an angel and it is worded as such:

And it came to pass, that the beggar died, and was carried by the <u>angels</u> into Abraham's bosom; the rich man died, and was buried.

Again this angel or angels are just talked about, but this time they do carry the poor man to heaven, and as you go along with this reading you will find out the rich man goes to a place that is very hot, I do believe they call it, HELL.

LUKE 20:36—Again this is Jesus talking to a crowd and the Sadducees ask him the question of what would happen to a women married to seven brothers (each at their own time) and each dying, but none having children by her. Who will she go with in heaven? The first husband or which of his brothers? This is how my Bible puts it in Jesus' word:

Neither can they die any more; for they are equal unto the <u>angels</u>; and are the children of god, being the children of the resurrection.

I want you to read that one more time slowly. Do you see where YOU will be "equal" to an angel if you repent and go to heaven? But it does <u>not</u> say you "will" be an angel, but "only equal" too an angel. Read all of the words when you read and take your time and study what you read. Again, if you are having trouble, talk with your Pastor about it, or a good Bible study teacher.

LUKE 22:43—This is when the disciples are sitting down to the Passover meal with Jesus and he is explaining what will happen to him, then they go to the mount of Olives and he starts to pray, telling the disciples to pray and do not go into temptation. The part with the angel is Verse 43, and is worded as such:

And there appeared an <u>angel</u> unto him from heaven, strengthening him.

And right after this is when Judas betrays Jesus, for six pieces of silver.

<u>LUKE 24:4</u>—This is during the time that the women came to the sepulcher to finish the job for burying Jesus, and they find the stone rolled back, and Jesus' body is not there. This is how it is worded in Luke:

<u>VERSE 4)</u>—*And it came to pass, as they were much perplexed thereabout, behold, <u>two men</u> stood by them in shining garments.* (These two men are angels).

<u>VERSE 23)</u>—*And when they found not his body, they came, saying, that they had also seen a vision of <u>angels</u>, which said that he was alive.*

<u>VERSE 37)</u>—Yes, this is worded as a spirit but also meaning angel. We would probably say ghost.

But they were terrified and affrighted, and supposed that they had seen a <u>spirit</u>.

<u>VERSE 39)</u>—*Behold my hands and my feet, that it is I myself, handle me, and see; for a <u>spirit</u>* (angel) *hath not flesh and bones, as ye see me have.*

While you are at it, remember to compare all four books of the gospels and compare them, and see what differences you can find between each author. It might be just a word, or slightly more, but to me it is very interesting to see what has been written over time and the slight changes from each.

<u>Note:</u> Remember, "Not one of the disciples" where at the sepulcher, only the women, and they told the disciples what happened and about the angels. So each disciple may have heard it this way and another heard it that way.

Book of John
Theme of this book is: Jesus the Son of God.
This book is the fourth and the last Gospel written by John to tell the people to believe in Jesus. From the beginning of the Gospel John tells that Jesus is God, stressing Jesus' relationship with God the Father. The Gospel centers on seven of Jesus' miracles and to prove his ministry Jesus called the people to have faith in him and promised eternal life and proved it by raising Lazarus from the grave. John also tells of the seven "I Am" statements, Jesus rendezvous with Nicodemus, the Samaritan woman, his upper room teachings, and the washing of the disciple's feet along with the great priestly prayer.

JOHN 1:51—This is when Jesus is talking to Nathanael after he has said that no good would come out of Nazareth. This is also at the end of chapter one when Jesus is finishing talking to Nathanael.

And he saith unto him, Verily, verily, I say unto you, Hereafter ye shall see heaven open, and the <u>angels</u> of God ascending and descending upon the Son of man.

JOHN 5:4—This is during the time that Jesus is going to the pool of Bethesda and comes across a crippled man trying to get to the pool to be healed, but others get their first, for this man has no one to help him. The pool is stirred up by an angel nearly daily and if you get their first you can be healed. This is how it is worded in my Bible:

For an <u>angel</u> went down at a certain season into the pool, and troubled (stirred) *the water: whosoever then first after* the troubling of the water stepped in was made whole of whatsoever disease he had.

This verse does not say very much about this angel, other than: He went down to stir up the waters; to me he would just be messenger angel.

JOHN 20:12-14—Again this is the story of Mary Magdalene coming to the sepulcher and finding the stone moved away and after telling some of the disciples they ran and looked in, when Mary Magdalene looked in, she then sees two angels, it is worded as such in my Bible:

VERSE 12)—*And seeth two angels in white sitting, the one at the head, and the other at the feet, where the body of Jesus had lain.*

VERSE 13)—*And they say unto her,* **Woman, why weepst thou?** *She saith unto them, because they have taken away my Lord, and I know not where they have laid him.*

VERSE 14)—*And when she had thus said, she turned herself back, and saw Jesus standing, and knew not it was him.*

Now these two angels, I believe, are just messenger angels for they are just telling Mary where Jesus is.

Now the book of John is not very big, and as you guessed we are through it already, so we will continue with the next book which is the book of Acts. Remember, if you are having a problem with a verse; please contact your pastor of your church, or a Bible study teacher. Thank you, make the pastor earn his money. (Maybe I should start running for the hills very soon, especially if I get more than one pastor unhappy with me for telling their flock to go to him with their questions).

The Book of Acts
The theme of this book is: The early church.
The author of this Book of Acts is Luke, and tells of when Jesus goes up to heaven and some of the questions they (the disciples) asked Jesus. Again this was written to Theophilus in a form of a letter and starts where the Gospels leave off, recording the early progress of the Gospel that the disciples took with them as they taught all around the Mediterranean world. Then Jesus after he spoke to them of the things to happen; told them that they had to wait in Jerusalem for God will fill them with the Holy Ghost, so they can preach the word of God in all countries. Below is the first mention of angels:

ACTS 1:9-11—I am starting one verse in front of the verse that mentions angels:

VERSE 9)—*And when he had spoken these things, while they beheld, he was taken up; and a cloud received him out of their site.* (This is Jesus going to heaven).

VERSE 10)—*And while they looked steadfastly toward heaven as he went up. Behold two men stood by them in white apparel.*

VERSE 11)—*Which also said,* **Ye men of Galilee, why stand ye gazing up into heaven, shall so come in like manner as ye have seen him go into heaven.**

Yes, this is talking about two angels, telling the disciples that Jesus will return the same way as he left earth. As I have said before you have to think when you read and study. How many of you would just read it and say it was two men, instead of angels?? These are just messenger angels, for they only tell of what is happening.

ACTS 2:2-4—In this section of Acts it is talking of the disciples being filled with the Holy Ghost: It is worded as such in my Bible:

VERSE 2)—*And suddenly there came a sound from heaven as of a <u>rushing mighty wind</u>, and it filled the house where they were sitting.*

VERSE 3)—*And there appeared unto them <u>cloven</u>* (Split in two) *<u>tongues like as of fire</u>, and sat upon each of them.*

VERSE 4)—*And they were all filled with the <u>Holy Ghost,</u> and began to speak with other tongues, as the <u>Spirit</u> gave them utterance.* (Way of speaking)

Do you remember what a rushing wind is, or a spirit? Look it up in the front of this book if you do not. Do you understand what "other tongues" are? In the verse listed here it means that the people were speaking in other languages, not from their tongue in the country they came from.

As I said in this book earlier, a spirit in the New Testament usually is a good thing, but you do have to be careful for some may work for Satan. This is a good spirit.

ACTS 5:19—This is when the high priest, (who was a Sadducees) came with his people and put the apostles in a common prison. This is what comes next:

VERSE 19)—*But the <u>angel</u> of the Lord by night opened the prison doors, and brought them forth, and said.*

VERSE 20)—**Go, stand and speak in the temple to the people all the words of life.**

Then after this, the high priest had the captain of the guard bring the apostles to the council, and had them whipped. But they still went on preaching about Jesus and God, throughout the land. Do you think that you could do something like the apostles are doing, and then get thrown in prison and beaten?

ACTS 7:30, 35, 53—This is telling of Moses after he fled Egypt, for killing a guard for killing an Israelite, after the guard was seen beating an Israelite. This is how it is worded in my Bible:

VERSE 30)—*And when forty years were expired,*(Gone by) *there appeared to him in the wilderness of mount Sina (Mt. Sinai) an angel of the Lord in a flame of fire in a bush.*

VERSE 35)—*This Moses whom they refused, saying, Who made you a ruler and a judge? The same God send to be a ruler and a deliverer by the hand of the angel which appeared to him in the bush.*

I guess that you know this but I will tell you anyway. The Israel people just kept going back to the time when it was, before they left Egypt. They just never seemed to learn what God has in store for them. This next verse is telling of what God has to say to the people, after they have Aaron build a golden calf to worship: This again is talking about Moses, and goes like this:

VERSE 38)—*This is he, that was in the church in the wilderness with the angel which spake (spoke) to him in the mount Sina,* (Mt. Sinai) *and with our fathers, who was received the lively oracles* (God given message) *to give unto us.*

VERSE 42)—*Then God turned, and gave them up to worship the host of heaven;*

There is more to that verse, but I only put this part down for you. It does not say an angel but only the host of heaven, which to me includes all of the angels, God, and Jesus. As you read this part of the Chapter, I want you to decide who is talking, Moses or God. Just read it slowly. Again I want to point out to you that the Bible can be confusing to some people, so read it slowly and concentrate on what you are reading.

VERSE 53)—*Who has received the law by the disposition* (nature) *of angels, and have not kept it.*

ACTS 8:26-29—This is when the apostles are going back to Jerusalem to preach their word about Jesus, and is worded as such:

Angels and the Angel of Light 131

VERSE 26)—*And the <u>angel</u> of the Lord spake* (spoke) *unto Philip, saying,* **Arise, and go toward the south unto the way that goeth** (goes) **down from Jerusalem unto** *Gaza,* **which is desert.**

These next two verses do not mention an angel but I put them in so you can follow better.

VERSE 27)—*And he arose and went; and behold, a man of Ethiopia, an eunuch* (a man who is not able to have sex with women, for his testicles where removed) *of great authority under Candace queen of the Ethiopians, who had the charge of all her treasure, and had come to Jerusalem to worship.*

VERSE 28)—*Was returning, and sitting in his chariot read* (reading) *Esalias* (Isaiah) *the prophet.*

VERSE 29)—*Then the <u>spirit</u> said unto Philip,* **Go near, and join thyself to this chariot.**

Philip let the eunuch read and then explained what was meant by what he read, and as they kept going they came to some water and Philip baptized the eunuch. Then it goes like this in verse 39.

VERSE 39)—*And when they were came up out of the water, the <u>Spirit of the Lord</u> caught away Philip, that the eunuch saw him no more; and he went on his way rejoicing.*

ACTS 10:3-7—This is about the centurion called Cornelius of a band called an Italian band (For this band only used the Greek version of the texts, which was a small group) who was a devout man, and had a vision which goes like so:

VERSE 3)—*He saw in a vision evidently about the ninth hour of the day an <u>angel</u> of God coming in to him, and saying unto him,* **Cornelius.**

VERSE 4)—*And when he looked on him, he was afraid, and said, What is it, Lord? And he said unto him,* **Thy prayers and thy alms are come up for a memorial before God.**

VERSE 5)—*And now send men to Joppa, and call for one Simon, whose surname is Peter.*

VERSE 6)—*He lodgeth* (lives) *with one Simon a tanner, whose house is by the sea side; and he shall tell thee what thou oughtest to do.*

VERSE 7)—*And when the angel which spake* (spoke) *unto Cornelius was departed,* (left the area) *he called two of his household servants, and a devout soldier of them that waited on him continually.*

Now we skip down to verse 19, but YOU MUST READ EVERYTHING IN BETWEEN. Thank you. This is while Peter is having a dream and is trying to figure out what the dream in about, that Cornelius' men came to the house. Nineteen is worded as such:

VERSE 19)—*While Peter thought on the vision, the spirit said unto him,* **Behold, three men seek thee.**

VERSE 20)—*Arise therefore, and get thee down, and go with them, doubting nothing; for I have sent them.*

Now as you read the rest of this chapter you should find Holy Ghost spoken of and a man of bright clothing spoken of. But that is all, it just speaks of them.

ACTS 12: 7-11, 15, 23—This is after Herod had killed James (the brother of John) he took Peter also and put him in prison with a guard chained to him on both sides to deal with later, This is how it is worded about the angel:

VERSE 7)—*And, behold the angel of the Lord came upon him, and a light shined in the prison; and he smote* (struck) *Peter on the side, and raised him up, saying,* **Arise up quickly.** *And his chains fell off from his hands.*

VERSE 8)—*And the angel said unto him,* **Gird** (put a belt on) **thyself, and bind** (tie) **on thy sandals.** *And so he did. And* *he saith unto him,* **Cast** (put) ***thy garment about thee, and follow me.***

VERSE 9)—*And he went out, and followed him; and wist* (thought) *not that it was true which was done by the <u>angel</u>, but thought he saw a vision.*

VERSE 10)—*When they were past the first and the second ward, they came unto the iron gate that leadeth* (leads) *unto the city; which opened to them of his own accord; and they went out, and passed on through on street; and forthwith the <u>angel</u> departed from him.*

VERSE 11)—*And when Peter was come to himself, he said, Now I know of a surety, that the Lord hath sent his <u>angel</u>, and hath delivered me out of the hand of Herod, and from all the expectation of the people of the Jews.*

Now in verse 15 it just mentions that it is his angel (They did not believe the girl and decided it had to be Peter's angel as they figured he was dead). Now the next item is when Herod is all dressed up as a king and starts talking to the people and the people say it is God talking to them, and Herod was gloating. Then it goes into the verse with the angel:

VERSE 23)—*And immediately the <u>angel</u> of the Lord smote* (struck) *him, because he gave not God the glory; and he was eaten of worms, and gave up the ghost.* (died)

I do believe that most of these angels are just messengers except the last one in verse twenty three, and that one I would call a Destroyer, and it could possibly be a Cherubim. I think I will stay with the destroyer angel.

ACTS 23:8 & 9—This is when Paul is brought before a Jewish council and they want to stone and beat him. But he realized that there were both Pharisees and Sadducees and were divided, for the Sadducees say that there is no resurrection. This is how it is worded in this verse:

VERSE 8)—*For the Sadducees say that there is no resurrection, neither <u>angel</u>, nor <u>spirit</u>; but the Pharisees confess* (acknowledge) *both.*

VERSE 9)—*And there arose a great cry; and the scribes that were of the Pharisees part arose, and strove, saying, We find no evil in this man; but if a <u>spirit</u> or an <u>angel</u> hath spoken to him, let us not fight against God.*

<u>ACTS 27 : 23-24</u>—This is when Paul is going to Italy and they are in shallow water and are afraid of hitting the rocks, (during a storm) and some abandon ship and are lost; Paul tells those on the ship that they will be okay. This is how it is worded about the angel:

VERSE 23)—*For there stood by me this night the <u>angel</u> of the God, whose I am, and whom I serve.*

VERSE 24)—*Saying,* **Fear not, Paul; thou must be brought before Caesar; and, lo, God hath given thee all them that sail with thee.**

All through these verse's, (Chapter 23, verse 8 through 24) the angels that are mentioned are all messenger angels.

The Book of Romans
(This is really worded: The Epistle of Paul to the Romans)
<u>The theme of this book is: God's righteousness.</u>

This book (or letter) is written to the Romans by Paul and is the longest and most precise aim of all of Paul's letters. He tells the theme in 1:16-17, that this Gospel is God's word for salvation for Jews and Gentiles, and shows us how our righteousness comes from God. He tells of the need for justification, through faith, because of sin, and then explains the results of being justified by faith in terms of both present practice and future hope. Then is the next three chapters Paul will signify his sorrow that many of his fellow Israelites have not followed the Gospels, and worries about the religious implications of this. Paul then concludes this letter by describing how the Gospel should affect ones everyday life.

Actually, there are no angels listed in this book written by Paul. Now you can read it to see if I am right or wrong, for it is like all the rest of the Bible, (meant to be read) read it all and prove me wrong. Thank you.

_____

_____

_____

Book of 1st Corinthians

Also titled: The First Epistle of Paul the Apostle to the Corinthians

The theme of this book is: Unity of the body.

Paul to me in this book is telling the people of Corinthians from Ephesus that Corinth was at the heart of the trade route and that they depended on trade, but it had a bad reputation for sexual immorality, corruption, and religious differences. The church that Paul had started their, was struggling with all of these problems and had started to split over various issues. This book tells of many of the practical questions that were dividing the church, questions on spiritual gifts, marriage, food offerings to idols, and the resurrection. Paul asks the Corinthians to come together and to give themselves completely over to the work of the Lord. Chapter thirteen contains a well know passage on the nature and importance of love.

There is only one mention of an angel in this book and it is worded as such:

1ˢᵗ CORINTIANS 11:10—*For this cause ought* (Be morally right) *the woman to have power on her head because of the angels.*

You just have to read this entire book of the Bible to understand what Paul is talking about. To me he is saying that a woman came from a man and should have a covering over her head, and be morally right. But the way he goes about describing what is what, it sounds like he is just going in circles. I know I will hear about this one, from somebody.

Another point in this book is in versus 22-24, not about angels but I know when you see the words you will scratch your head and they are side by side in verse 22; those words are Anathema which is: "recipient of a curse". But when you find Maranatha it is listed as: "Our Lord Come". When you read all of the verse, SLOWLY, he is cursing those that do not love Jesus, but then saying Jesus is coming. Then read verse 23 and 24. (Those two words are from the Aramaic language, which Jesus spoke most of the time.

___
___
___

The Book of 2ⁿᵈ Corinthians

Also the title is: The Second Epistle of Paul the Apostle to the Corinthians

The theme of this book is: Paul defends his ministry.

This letter by Paul is describing believers to come together as one, to be unified with Paul in ministry. Paul's opponents are saying he cannot be a true Apostle as he suffers so much, but Paul tells them that Jesus' strength is what they should talk about, not his. This letter also includes Paul's stirring views on the Gospels, reassuring the people about holy living, and instructions on giving.

In this book I cannot remember any angels listed, but as you read it you should make sure that I am still in my right mind, I could have missed one, as I am getting older every day; and I have not figured out a way to turn the clock back a few years, yet.

It does say spirit a couple of times but that meaning is, like the "Spirit of the Lord".

Book of Galatians

The title also is: The Epistle of Paul the Apostle to the Galatians

The theme of this book is: Salvation by faith alone.

In this letter, Paul, is telling the Galatians that the old method of teaching; is that if you keep the laws of God you will be accepted by God, and began with a defense of his authority and made it clear that all believers, Jew and Gentile alike, would enjoy complete salvation in Jesus Christ. Paul shows how knowledge and believing in Jesus leads to genuine sovereignty and godly living. The point of this book is that a person is not excused by performing the Old Testament Laws, but through faith in Jesus Christ.

GALATIONS 3: 19—*Wherefore then serveth the law? It was added because of transgressions, till the seed should come to whom the promise was made; and it was ordained by angels in the hand of the mediator.*

What he is saying is that, we were given the law and were to follow the law, until Jesus came; and therefore the law was our school master to bring us unto Christ, that we be justified by faith.

He is not saying to forget the law, but you must believe in Jesus, and then you will have faith.

This is all there is about angels in this book.

The book of Ephesians
Also called: The Epistle of Paul the Apostle to the Ephesians
The theme of this book is: Becoming mature believers.

This Book (or letter) of the Bible by Paul, to the churches around Ephesus, is to display the extent of God's plans for all humanity, for Jews and Gentiles together. This is the mystery of God, concealed for ages, but now made known through Jesus Christ. The first three chapters make clear of what Christians believe, revealing the remarkable riches of God's grace in Jesus. Dead sinners are made alive and gain eternal salvation "by grace—through Christ." The last three chapters tell of the involvement of God's grace for the church, for individuals, and for families. The second section comes to a culmination with a command to stand firm with God against Satan.

The angels listed in this book are:

EPHESIANS 1:21—*Far above all principality, and power, and might, and dominion, and every name that is named, not only in this world, but also in that which is to come;*

Now if you do not remember what these four underlined words are; look them up in the front of this book. Are they good angels or bad angels??? Now re-read this verse and how does it start; does it not start with the words FAR ABOVE ALL? It is saying that Jesus will be above all of them, so if they are good or bad angels they will have to deal with Jesus if they harm humans and it will be that way in the next world.

EPHESIANS 3:10—*To the intent that now unto the <u>principalities</u> and <u>powers</u> in heavenly places might be known by the church the manifold* (many and various) *wisdom of God.*

Again, are these good angels or are they bad angels? Does it not say in heavenly places? This is what you have to be careful of, for one may mean good and another may mean bad. You have to study all the verses around what you are reading to understand that verse. Again this is just a mention of angels, where they do nothing and say nothing.

I do believe that this is all the angels listed in this book. I know it says spirit but I do believe it was meant to be the Spirit of God.

Book of Philippians

Another name is: The Epistle of Paul the Apostle to the Philippians

<u>The theme of this book is: The Joy of knowing Christ.</u>

This book was written by Paul to the Philippi people while Paul was in prison, thanking them for a gift sent to him. He tells them that the one who brought the gift has recovered from an illness and would be returning. He mentions being gratified in any circumstances, telling them of his problems in prison. He was overjoyed to hear that people where hearing about Jesus, even if some where preaching the gospel for the wrong reason, and to be a servant just as Jesus was when He "made himself nothing" and became a man.

Again there is no mention of angels in this book, and if you read it (I hope) that you will read and study it, as you read. Then if any questions just ask your pastor or Bible group leader. (Woops—those pastors will be looking for me, especially if they cannot answer the question.)

___

Book of Colossians

Also called: The Epistle of Paul the Apostle to the Colossians

The theme of this book is: Complete in Christ.

This letter (Book) written by Paul to the church in Colossae telling of false preaching, such as rules about eating and drinking, rules of religious festivals, and promoting of angel worshiping. Paul tells the people to leave their sin behind and to live a godly way, keeping Jesus as the head of the church.

There is not too much about angels in this book, and it will mean that you will have to read and make sure I am right. Again, you will have to do a little looking up of items so you are right (or wrong) as you read.

COLOSSIANS 1:16—*For by him were all things created, that are in heaven, and that are in earth, visible and invisible, whether they be <u>thrones</u> or <u>dominions</u>, or <u>principalities</u>, or <u>powers</u>: all things were created by him, and for him.*

Paul is just trying to tell the people that God created "all" things, bad or good, for himself. I do hope you looked these four underlined words up in the front of this book. Why did

God create bad things? Only He has the answer, but He did it for a reason, and that reason we must figure out.

COLOSSIANS 2:10—*And ye are complete in him, which is the head of all <u>principality</u> and <u>power</u>;*

To me it says that if you are completely under the faith of Jesus, then you also will be up and along with the principalities and powers, but I do not think it means higher than they. I could be very wrong on that one as I cannot wrap my finger around it completely. That must mean "God has something for me to learn" and I have to come back to this book and re-read it more than once, until I do figure it out. But I will continue on with this book and will come back later, unless it is something very important, then God will make sure I do it TODAY.

COLOSSIANS 2:18—*Let no man beguile you of your reward in a voluntary humility and worshipping of <u>angels</u>, intruding into those things which he hath not seen, vainly puffed up by his fleshy mind.*

I want you to look up these two words and then re-read this sentence—vainly—puffed. Does it read differently?

All this is saying is the one thing NOT to do; "do not worship angels" or let any man deceive you into worshipping angels. Just be very careful as there are a lot of people who are under the influence of Satan (Who is an angel), and do not be mislead by them.

Here is a little humor for you to read and relax a little before going on with this book.

God's left hand

Grampa Ed

Little Bobby was spending the weekend with his grandmother. His grandmother decided to take him to the park on Saturday morning. It had been snowing all night and everything was beautiful.

His grandmother remarked…"doesn't it look like an artist painted this scenery? Did you know that God painted it just for you?"

Bobby said, "Yes, God did it and he did it left handed."

This confused the grandmother a bit, and she asked him "What makes you think he painted it with his left hand?"

"Well," said Bobby, "we learned in Sunday School last week that Jesus sits on God's right hand."

Dear God letters:
Dear God,
Instead of letting people die and having to make new ones, why don't you keep the ones you have now?—Cindy

Dear God,
Who draws the lines around countries?—Nan

Dear God,
Why is Sunday school on Sunday? I thought it was supposed to be a day of rest.—Tom

CHAPTER SEVEN

GOOD ANGELS OF THE BIBLE BOOKS; 1ST THESSALONIANS, 2ND THESSALONIANS, 1ST TIMOTHY, 2ND TIMOTHY, TITUS, PHILEMON, HEBREWS

Book 1st. Thessalonians
Also know as: The First Epistle of Paul the Apostle to the Thessalonians
<u>The theme of this book is: Steadfast in the Lord.</u>
This is a letter from Paul to the people of the church in Thessalonica, encouraging new believers and to remind them of the coming of the Lord. Paul had to send Timotheus (Timothy) there, for he had to leave that area for the dislike of the Jewish people, and upon Timotheus's (Timothy's) return with good news of their faith he wrote this letter. I want you to know that most of the people here are gentiles.

I do believe that there is only one place in this book that mention angels, which is:

<u>1st THESSALONIANS 4:16</u>—*For the Lord himself shall descend from heaven with a shout, with the voice of the <u>archangel</u>, and with the trump of God; and the dead in Christ shall rise first.*

All this is saying is, that when Jesus returns, he will descend from heaven with a shout which will sound like the archangel, and the sound of God's trumpets, and those that have passed away with Jesus in their heart, will be the first to rise from the dead. (I have also heard that the word trump is called the winning hand, but I prefer God's trumpets.)

Now spirit is mentioned, but is the spirit of the Lord, and "quench not the spirit". To me this is meaning, keep the spirit of Jesus and do not let it cool down, do not your let the flame burn out.

___

Book—2nd. Thessalonians

Also known as: The Second Epistle of Paul the Apostle to the Thessalonians

The theme of this book is: Understand the day of the Lord.

This book (letter) is when Paul wrote to the church of Thessalonica that he was pleased with their faith and their love for one another, even while being persecuted. Paul tells the people that God will repay their persecutors and the people were worried that Jesus had already returned, so Paul tells them not to be alarmed, and reminded them not to be idle, saying, "if anyone is not willing to work, let them not eat."

Again this is a letter from Paul to the Thessalonians and there is only one place that I have found that mention's an angel. This is how it is worded:

2nd. THESSALONIANS 1:7—*And to you who are troubled rest with us, when the Lord Jesus shall be revealed from heaven with his mighty <u>angels.</u>*

Paul is telling the people that although they are being persecuted, they should have love for one another.

___

Book of 1st Timothy

Titled also: The First Epistle of Paul the Apostle to Timothy

The theme of this book is: Church leadership.

In the book of Timothy, angels are mentioned twice to the best of my knowledge. The book itself tells this; Paul (As he is getting older) wrote to Timothy who is like a son to Paul, and is giving some advice about false teachers, and instructed Timothy on church leadership, proper worshipping, qualifications for elders and deacons, and how to treat individual members within the congregation.

These are the verses that mention angels:

1st TIMOTHY 3:16—*And without controversy great is the mystery of godliness: God was manifest* (Appeared) *in the flesh, justified in the <u>Spirit</u>, seen of <u>angels</u>, preached unto the Gentiles, believed on in the world, received up into glory.*

I do hope that you know that Paul here is talking about Jesus which is done very quickly, with few words.

The other verse is as such:

1st TIMOTHY 5:21—*I charge thee before God, and the Lord Jesus Christ, and the elect <u>angels</u>, that thou observe these things without preferring one before another, doing nothing by partiality.*

This is just how it is worded; do not prefer one person over another, no partiality. This next verse is not pertaining to angels, but you should read this verse in 1st Timothy 5:23—I thought it was interesting to note that people in the days of Paul had health problems and Timothy must have had some stomach problems. This is how it is worded:

1st TIMOTHY 5:23—*Drink no longer water, but use a little wine for thy stomach's sake and thine* (your) *infirmities.* (Minor illness)

I wonder if it was from polluted water or maybe he was getting an ulcer. We will never know.

Book of 2nd Timothy

Also called: The Second Epistle of Paul the Apostle to Timothy

The theme of this book is: Personal encouragement.

In this letter to Timothy; as Paul was facing execution in a Roman jail, was telling Timothy to be bold in his ministry, to have endurance and faithfulness, even in the face of false teachings. He tells Timothy to have sound doctrine and scripture as it is inspired by God. He also mentions that the older members must be willing to pass on their knowledge of scriptures to the young.

There are no angels in this book, but if you do find one, PLEASE let me know. Thanks.

Book of Titus

Also called: The Epistle of Paul to Titus.

The theme of this book is: Conduct for church living.

This letter by Paul is very short to Titus but it is telling him the "Conduct for Church Living". It encourages Titus to prevail over opposition from the ungodly and the legalists (Interpretation of the religious or moral code) within the congregation. He also tells how to establish elders and what type people they should be. All Christians should live a self-controlled, upright, godly life, until Jesus returns.

Again there are no angels in this letter to Timothy, but read it anyway. Thanks.

Book of Philemon
Also called: The Epistle of Paul to Philemon
The theme of this book is: Christian love and forgivness.

This letter from Paul to Philemon is a very short, short letter, written by Paul as he still is in prison and the theme you can say is; Christian love and forgiveness. Philemon had a slave named Onesimus, who stole from Philemon and then fled. While Paul was in prison he somehow meets the slave and converts him. Then sends Onesimus back to Philemon appealing to him to accept the slave back into his house, but not as a slave, but as a brother in Christ, and Paul also offers to pay Onesimus' debt to Philemon.

Again there are no angels listed in this letter (or Book).

Book of Hebrews
Also called: The Epistle to the Hebrews
The theme of this book is: Christ is superior.

Hebrews: This book is written by an unknown author and the theme is simply; Christ is Superior. This book reminds us that we should live "not" in the past, but tells us that Jesus is speaking to us, who is, the exact imprint (image) of God. There will be salvation for all who believe, and we should imitate the way Jesus lived.

The angels in this book are as follows:

HEBREWS 1:4—*Being made so much better than the <u>angels</u>, as he hath by inheritance obtained a more excellent name than they.*

HEBREWS 1:5—*For unto which of the <u>angels</u> said he at any time,* **<u>Thou art my Son, this day have I begotten thee? And again, I will be to him a Father, and he shall be to me a son.</u>**

HEBREWS 1:6—*And again, when he bringeth* (brings) *in the firstbegotten* (first born) *into the world, he saith,* **<u>And let all the angels of God worship him.</u>**

HEBREWS 1:7—*And of the angels he saith,* **<u>Who maketh his angels spirits, and his ministers a flame of fire.</u>**

HEBREWS 1:13—*But to which of the <u>angels</u> said he at any time,* **<u>Sit on my right hand, until I make thine enemies thy footstool?</u>**

HEBREWS 1:14—**<u>Are they not all ministering spirits, sent forth to minister for them who shall be heirs of salvation?</u>**

All the above you should read again; who is talking, God or Jesus? At first as I read it, to me it is Jesus talking about what God did for him, and will do for us if we believe in him; but studying this more, I have decided that it is God telling about what he has done for all of us, then and today. I know some scholar will say NO WAY, but that is the way I read it. Now this is being told by the author who is unknown, but knows a lot about Jesus.

HEBREWS 2:2—*For if the word spoken by <u>angels</u> was steadfast, and every transgression* (wrongdoing) *and disobedience received a just recompence* (compensation) *of reward;*

HEBREWS 2:5—*For unto the <u>angels</u> hath he not put in subjection the world to come, whereof we speak.*

HEBREWS 2:7—*Thou madest* (made) *him a little lower than the angels; thou crowndest* (crowns) *him with glory and honour, and didst set him over the works of thy hands.*

HEBREWS 2:9—*But we see Jesus, who was made a little lower than the angels for the suffering of death, crowned with glory and honour; that by grace of God should taste death for every man.*

HEBREWS 2:16—*For verily he took not on him, the nature of angels; but he took on him the seed of Abraham.* (Jesus was not an angel but was human from the line of Abraham)

HEBREWS 12:22—*But ye are come unto Mount Sion,* (Zion) *and unto the city of the living God, the heavenly Jerusalem, and to an innumerable company of angels.*

HEBREWS 13:2—*Be not forgetful to entertain strangers; for thereby some have entertained angels unawares.* (If you entertain a stranger, do it with pleasure for it may be an angel, but just beware it is not a fallen angel)

Most of the angels talked about in Hebrews are only mentioned for what they have done, but they do not do anything or say anything.

Book of James
Also known as: The Epistle of James
The theme of this book is: Faith that works.

The Book of James reminds us how to live by true faith, having patience, biting ones tongue, obeying God's will and living sensibly for Jesus. You can say it is the Proverbs of the New Testament; and is thought to be written by Jesus' brother James.

There are no angels listed in this book. But just read it for your information that "you need".

___

Book of 1st. Peter
Also called: The First Epistle of Peter
The theme of this book is: Sharing Jesus' suffering.

This is Peter's Apostle of Hope, whose message is to trust God and love obediently, no matter what occurs. You will have suffering here and there, but if you are steadfast in your belief in Jesus you will have your inheritance in Christ when he comes again, and he will take you to heaven.

The angels listed in this book are as follows:

1st PETER 1:12—*Unto whom it was revealed, that not unto themselves, but unto us they did minister the things, which are now reported unto you by them that have preached the gospel unto you with the Holy Ghost sent down from heaven; which things the angels desire to look into.*

1st PETER 3:22—*Who is gone into heaven, and is on the right hand of God; angels and authorities and powers being made subject to him.*

Again the angels are just in a letter and do nothing or say anything; it is just saying Jesus is in charge of them.

That is all on angels in this book of Peter.

___

Book of 2nd Peter
Also called: The Second Epistle of Peter
The theme of this book is: Guard against false teachers.

Peter wrote this letter just prior to his death, from a Roman prison. Christian truth was being taught in versions that were being twisted. He tells the readers that the Gospels are like a lamp, shining in a dark place. People do not believe that Jesus would return some day in the final judgment. Peter reminds them that God destroyed the world once with water and he will do it again, but this time in fire; so we must live in holiness and in goodness as we wait Jesus' return.

You should read this complete letter (book), and it is not too long, so understand what is being said about the angels, which is in the two verses below:

2ⁿᵈ PETER 2:4—*For if God spared not the <u>angels</u> that sinned, but cast them down to hell, and delivered them into chains of darkness, to be reserved unto judgment.*

Peter is telling you that God has spared many a person over the centuries, even angels, but some go to hell until judgment day, then they will have their say before final judgment. This tells about the angels that are following Satan.

2ⁿᵈ PETER 2:11—*Whereas <u>angels</u>, which are greater in power and might, bring not railing* (false) *accusations against them before the Lord.*

I did not underline the words power and might, for the way it is written it is saying that the angels "are" greater "in" power and might, for they are just stronger. Here the words power and might do not pertain to fallen angels, or angels.

That is all on angels in this letter, but as you read 2ⁿᵈ Peter take notice of <u>verse 8 in chapter 3</u>, and I will put only the last half down here.—*Be not ignorant of this one thing, that one day is with the Lord as a thousand years, and a thousand years as one day.*—Now you know where it is when somebody mentions this.

CHAPTER EIGHT

GOOD ANGELS OF THE BIBLE.
BOOKS OF 1ST JOHN, 2ND JOHN, 3RD JOHN, JUDE, REVELATION

Since these three are small books (letters), I have decided to group them together to make it easier for you the reader. All three books do not say anything about angels, but I will give you a quick overview of the books. (But I still want you to read each one). **Every day of your life, you should read a little of the Bible.**

1st John—The theme of this book is:Fellowship with God.

John wrote this message to the people of the churches in Asia Minor (which today is Turkey). He tells the people the truth about the incarnations (the truth of Jesus being born a human but was from God the Father), as there were many falsehoods from teachers who denied the divinity of Jesus. He tells them that we should have sound doctrine, love, and obedience or we are not true Christians. And if we have love for one another as sisters and brothers in Christ, and follow the items above and live a holy life, we will have salvation.

2nd John—The theme of this book is: Avoid false teachers.

Like 1st John, he warns us of false teachers, but his letter written to a Christian woman and her family, dealing with hospitality. The False teachers were using people's hospitality to gain control of John's congregations. John warns of opening your home up to these teachers, who would try to destroy ones faith, and that sound doctrine will bring meaningful fellowship.

Now I want you to really think on this message that is next, as it is happening every day right here in America today (and elsewhere), just like it did back in the time of John.

3rd John—The theme of this book is: Christian fellowship.

John wrote this letter to Gaius, who was a member of one of his congregations. He approved that Gaius was living as the Apostles taught, for he had welcomed missionaries into his home. John condemned Diotrephes, who had refused the missionaries, and who also slandered John. "This letter shows how **trivial** things can divide a congregation" if they do not live by God's word and love. And this letter (book) is only thirteen verses long.

___

Book of Jude
Also called: The Epistle of Jude
The theme of this book is: Contend for the faith.

This is another very short letter or book, and Jude is believed to be the half brother of Jesus. He was warning the people to whom he wrote this letter to, that there were some in the church corrupting the grace of God and denying Jesus. Jude also condemned these ungodly persons who reject authority and who defile the flesh. He urges those that are Christians to continue in godliness and love toward the ungodly, to turn them to Christianity and to snatch them from the fire. The angels listed in this book are as follows:

JUDE 1—Chapter one, verse 6 (six) is telling about fallen angels, with the others being the Good angels of the Bible.

Jude here is just talking about them and what God has done to them, so I put them down here but they really are both type of angels. Confusing, yes, but I think it will make it easier for you when we start on the fallen angels.

JUDE 1:6—*And the <u>angels</u> which kept not heir first estate* (heaven), *but left their own habitation* (surroundings), *he hath reserved in everlasting chains under darkness unto the judgment of the great day.* (These are all fallen angels) JUDE 1:9—*Yet <u>Michael the archangel</u>, when contending with the devil he disputed* (argued) *about the body of Moses, durst* (dared) *not bring against him a railing* (false) *accusation, but said, The Lord rebuke thee.*

JUDE 1:14—*And Enoch also, the seventh from Adam, prophesied of these, saying, Behold, the Lord cometh with ten thousands of his <u>saints</u>.* (Or angels)

JUDE 1:25—*To the only wise God our savior, be glory and majesty, dominion and power now and ever. Amen.*

Yes, the words dominion and power are listed, but I did not underline them as this is just telling us that God is the one with the glory, majesty, dominion and power. This does not pertain to angels, which is why I keep harping on reading slow so you get the correct meaning of the writing in the Bible.

Book of Revelation
The theme of this book is: Last things.

The Last book of the Bible was written by John while he was on the Island of Patmos, while he was in exile. This is his revelation as told to him by Jesus, and as he testifies of what is to happen, he puts it down on paper in letters to the seven churches. In these letters it contains commendation, criticism, and comfort. Then he changes his writing to tell of his vision of judgment on the wicked, with the church in distress, but also assuring the final triumph of Jesus bringing in the new Heaven and a new Earth, where God will reign for all eternity. We will go into the angels in Revelation here, but I do not want you to read any part of this book until you read all of the other books of the Bible FIRST. <u>Note: A lot of people can not understand this book and some actually become afraid after reading this book.</u> I do believe that is because they did not read and understand what was in the Bible "before" this book.

This is a book of prophesy of what may happen, today, tomorrow, or next month, or next year. Only God knows when and how he will send Jesus down to earth, but this time all sin and sinners, will be gone, along with Satan and his fallen angels. I suppose if you are a sinner you have a right to be afraid after reading this book.

STOP:

Do not go farther until you read "all of the books of the Bible up to" Revelation. If you read this book before you know what all the other books are about, you will be thoroughly confused and may never want to read the bible again. This book you must remember is all PROPHECY (predictions) from John, who claims he received it from Jesus, and this may happen to all of us in the future. Yes, I do believe it will happen, but when, how, why, where, is up to God only. All I can tell you is to be prepared, for tomorrow may never come for some people of earth.

This is the list of good angels in Revelation: I will just list the chapter and verse or verses that pertain to them and will show you what they say, do or are:

REVELATION 1:1—*The revelation of Jesus Christ, which God gave unto him, to shew* (show) *unto his servants things which must shortly come to pass; and he sent and signified it by his <u>angel</u> unto his servant John:*

This angel is a good angel and is a messenger angel, as he just tells John of the things to come.

REVELATION 1:20—(This is Jesus saying this to John). *The mystery of the seven stars which thou sawest (saw) in my right hand, and the seven golden candlesticks. The seven stars are the <u>angels</u> of the seven churches; and the seven candlesticks which thou sawest are the seven churches.*

This is just saying that the stars in Jesus' hand are the angels that will be with the seven churches. There is no indication of what type an angel they are.

REVELATION 2:1—All through this chapter it tells of the angels of the church; then tells the name of the church. All it is saying is to write to the angel of each church, and the way it is worded I will say they are the leaders of each church, not really angels. This also goes into chapter three.

REVELATION 4:6-9—This does not sound like angels, but thinking back on what two others have seen and spoken of; I believe they could be angels but are actually called beasts. I am only going to put verse eight down here, but I want you to read all the others I have listed at the beginning of this chapter. The one book that does talk of angels similar to this is in Ezekiel but they also have wheels. Now I question the scholars: are these "another" type of Angel, and if so, what are they? If it is another type, I believe that takes it up to fourteen different types.

REVELATION 4:8—*And the four <u>beasts</u> had each of them six wings about him; and they were full of eyes within; and* *they rest not day or night, saying,* **Holy, holy, holy, Lord God Almighty, which was, and is, and is to come.**

REVELATION 4:9—*And when those <u>beasts</u> give glory and honour and thanks to him that sat on the throne, who liveth for ever and ever.*

REVELATION 4:10—*The four and twenty elders fall down before him and sat on the throne; and worship him that liveth for ever and ever, and cast their crowns before the throne, saying,*

Now verse ten says four and twenty elders and that is what it is; not the four beasts, so be careful when you read, please. I put this verse in to see if you were thinking four beasts/or four and twenty elders. As I said earlier, one word can throw your reading and studying way off the track.

I do hope you remember the angels that were like a beast with four faces and six wings, and these are so close, I am going to call them angels.

REVELATION 5:2—*And I saw a <u>strong angel</u> proclaiming with a loud voice,* **Who is worthy to open the book, and to loose** (untie, takeoff) *the seals thereof?*

This angel should be a little higher than a regular angel as he has control of the book with seven seals.

REVELATION 5:6—*And I beheld, and lo, in the midst of the throne and of the <u>four beasts</u>, and in the midst of the elders, stood a Lamb as it had been slain, having seven eyes, which are the seven Spirits of God sent forth into the earth.*

REVELATION 5:8—*And when he had taken the book, the <u>four beasts</u> and four and twenty elders fell down before the Lamb, having every one of them harps, and golden vials full of odours, which are the prayers of saints.*

REVELATION 5:11—*And I beheld, and I heard the voice of many <u>angels</u> round about the throne and the <u>beasts</u> and the* *elders; and the number of them was ten thousand times ten thousand and thousands of thousands.*

Do you think you can count that high? That is a lot of angels and if they sang together it should be beautiful music, maybe a little loud, but beautiful music anyway.

This verse I am only going to put part of it in as I figure by know you should be reading everything in the Bible.

REVELATION 5:14—*And the four beast said, Amen.*

I will do the same with all of the beasts below, only part of the verse, I want you to learn, not to be given everything. You have to learn to stand on your own two feet. If you do not understand it the first time, come back later and read it again after you have put some thought to it. Then if you are lost go to your pastor or Bible study teacher.

REVELATION 6:1—*And I saw when the Lamb opened one of the seals, and I heard, as it were the noise of thunder, one of the <u>four beasts</u> saying,* **Come and see.**

So the beasts were very loud when they spoke as it was like "thunder". This is where all of the different colored horses are released, first a WHITE horse, then a RED horse, then a BLACK horse, and the last one being a PALE horse. Now as you read, go slow, and try to remember what each horse is for.

REVELATION 6:3—*And when he opened the second seal, I heard the second <u>beast</u> say,* **Come and see.**

REVELATION 6:5—*And when he had opened the third seal, I heard the third <u>beast</u> say,* **Come and see.**

REVELATION 6:7—*And when he had opened the fourth seal, I heard the fourth <u>beast</u> say,* **Come and see.**

Now it will go back to regular angels, but we must keep an eye out for good angels and fallen angels, so be careful as you read.

REVELATION 7:1—*And after these things I saw four <u>angels</u> standing on the four corners of the earth, holding the four winds of the earth, that the wind should not blow on the earth, nor on the sea, nor on any given tree.*

REVELATION 7:2—*And I saw another <u>angel</u> ascending from the east, having the seal of the living God: and he cried with a loud voice to the four <u>angels</u>, to whom it was given to hurt the earth and the sea.*

In the above section of the Bible, it tells of all the twelve tribes of Israel being sealed with the "servants of our God" on their foreheads; which equals a hundred and forty and four thousand of all the Israelites. Now as you read it will tell you from each tribe how many was sealed. Then it will tell you also that a great number, which no man could number of all nations, kindred's, people and tongues, dressed in white robes, and palms in their hands. Do you think you are sinless enough to be one of them? If not you best start repenting.

REVELATION 7:11—*And all the angels stood around about the throne, and about the elders and the four beasts, and fell before the throne on their faces, and worshipped God.*

To me the next few verses are very important as it is telling you (and me) that we will serve God day and night in heaven in his temple, and that God will dwell with us.

REVELATION 8:2—*And I saw the seven <u>angels</u> which stood before God; and to them were given seven trumpets.*

REVELATION 8:3—*And another <u>angel</u> came and stood at the altar; having a golden censer;* (container for burning incense) *and there was given him much incense, that he should offer it with the prayers of all saints upon the golden altar which was before the throne.*

REVELATION 8:4—*And the smoke of the incense, which came with the prayers of the saints, ascended up before God out of the <u>angels</u> hand.*

REVELATION 8:5—*And the <u>angel</u> took the censer, and filled it with fire of the altar, and cast it into the earth; and there were voices, and thundering, and lightnings, and an earthquake.*

REVELATION 8:6—*And the seven <u>angels</u> which had the seven trumpets prepared themselves to sound.*

REVELATION 8:7—*The first <u>angel</u> sounded, and there followed hail and fire mingled with blood, and they were cast upon the earth; and the third part of trees was burnt up, and all green grass was burnt up.*

REVELATION 8:8—*And the second <u>angel</u> sounded, and as it were a great mountain burning with fire was cast in the sea; and the third part of the sea became blood.*

(Verse 9 goes with this, which I put down for you)

REVELATION 8:9—*And the third part of the creatures which were in the sea, and had life, died; and the third part of the ships were destroyed.*

REVELATION 8:10—*And the third <u>angel</u> sounded, and there fell a great star from heaven, burning as it were a lamp, and it fell upon the third part of the rivers, and upon the fountain of waters.*

Now read what comes next (in your Bible) in verse eleven. The star is called wormwood and what did it do? Just read slowly, so you understand, it is easy as long as you read slow, and study as you read. (For the people that cannot figure it out: the star goes into the water and makes the water bitter and many men die from drinking the water).

REVELATION 8:12—*And the fourth <u>angel</u> sounded, and the third part of the sun was smitten,* (affected disastrously) *and the third part of the moon, and the third part of the stars; so as the third part of them was darkened, and the day shone not for a third part of it, and the night likewise.*

REVELATION 8:13—*And I beheld, and heard an <u>angel</u> flying through the midst of heaven, saying with a loud voice,* **Woe, woe, woe, to the inhabitors of the earth by reason of the other voices of the trumpet of the three angels, which are yet to sound!**

REVELATION 9:1—*And the fifth <u>angel</u> sounded, and I saw a star fall from heaven unto the earth; and to him was given the key of the bottomless pit.*

Now I want you to take your time reading and studying all of chapter nine, as it will tell of the scorpions that will plaque humans on earth, that do not have the seal (mark) of the Lord on their foreheads. Now I will list verse eleven here for you:

REVELATION 9:11—*And they had a king over them, which is the <u>angel</u> of the bottomless pit, whose name in the Hebrew tongue is Abaddon, but in the Greek tongue has his name Apollyon.*

REVELATION 9:13—*And the sixth <u>angel</u> sounded, and I heard a voice from the four horns, of the golden altar which is before God,*

REVELATION 9:14—*Saying to the sixth <u>angel</u> which had the trumpet,* **Loose** (Let go) **the four angels which are bound in the great river Euphrates.**

REVELATION 9:15—*And the four angels were loosed, which were prepared for the hour, and a day, and a month, and a year, for to slay the third part of men.*

Now I do believe that the angels with the trumpets are higher than messenger angels so I would say they would be captains over other angels or a group of angels. The other angels, that are doing the killing of those without God's Seal on them, are destroyer angels. Just read as I said earlier and study as you read, and if you are having problems, talk to your pastor or the Bible study leader.

REVELATION 10:1—*And I saw another mighty angel come down from heaven, clothed with a cloud; and a rainbow was upon his head, and his face was as it were the sun, and his feet as pillars of fire;*

As I read the rest of this section it tells of the seven thunders, and what the seven thunders are, and believed by some scholars to be the voice of God. What interests me is that John is told not to write these down; to seal them up. So I wonder; would it be too much for us to learn what will be coming next? Whatever it is, maybe I would be better off not knowing, but I sort of have an inquisitive mind. But as I look through here again, I notice it says that they had uttered "their" voices, so this is NOT God as I had thought earlier, could they be elders, saints, what? Now I am going to have to come back later and really do some studying on this. Of course some scholar may let me know so I can understand this. As I have said before, the bible can be confusing, mysterious, etc. And if you do not study what is written it can lead you astray, down a path that is not the right path.

REVELATION 10:5—*And the angel which I saw stand upon the sea and upon the earth lifted up his hand to heaven.*

REVELATION 10:7—*But in the days of the voice of the seventh angel, when he shall begin to sound, the mystery of God should be finished, as he hath declared to his servants the prophets.*

REVELATION 10:8—*And the voice which I heard from heaven spake* (spoke) *to me again, and said;* **Go take the little book which is open in the hand of the angel which standeth** (is standing) **upon the sea and upon earth.**

REVELATION 10:9—*And I went unto the angel, and said unto him, Give me the little book.* **And he said unto me, Take it, and eat it up; and it shall make thy belly bitter; but it shall be in thy mouth sweet as honey.**

REVELATION 10:10—*And I took the little book out of the angel's hand, and ate it up; and it was in my mouth sweet as honey, and as soon as I had eaten it, my belly was bitter.*

Then the angel tells John that he must go and prophesy again, before many people, countries, tongues, and kings.

REVELATION 11:1—*And there was given me a reed like unto a rod; and the angel stood, saying,* **Rise, and measure the temple of God, and the altar, and them that worship therein.**

Just think of the size of your church including the area for the congregation, and that will take care of what the words mean at the end of the sentence, "and them that worship therein". I just want you to read and remember to study, look items up, or ask your pastor, or Bible class instructor for help if lost. Just remember this is the start of the "end of times": so some of it may be a little frightening for some people.

REVELATION 11:15—*And the seventh angel sounded; and there were great voices in heaven, saying, The kingdoms of this world are become the kingdoms of our Lord, and of his Christ; and he shall reign for ever and ever.*

Just read the rest of this chapter and do as I have told you earlier, thanks.

Now when you start chapter twelve take your time reading; as you will find the first mention of a woman "in" heaven. The dragon is Satan or the Angel of Light. This is the next part of it as I have put some of it next. Again if lost ask your pastor or Bible class leader.

REVELATION 12:7—*And there was war in heaven; <u>Michael</u> and his <u>angels</u> fought against the dragon; and the dragon fought and his angels.*

I hope you noticed I did not underline the angel which is the last word of that paragraph, for they are all of the fallen angels. I will save all the fallen angels for reading in the next part of this book. This is when Michael defeats Satan and all his fallen angels and they are taken out of heaven. Now read the rest of Chapter twelve and then thirteen and start fourteen and then we will be back to good angels for a bit.

REVELATION 14:6—*And I saw another <u>angel</u> fly in the midst of heaven, having the everlasting gospel to preach unto them that dwell on the earth, and every nation, and kindred* (family/closeness) *and tongue, and people.*

REVELATION 14:8—*And there followed another <u>angel</u>, saying,* **Babylon is fallen, is fallen, that great city, because she made all nations drink of the wine of the wrath of her fornication.** (Sexual sin)

REVELATION 14:9—*And the third <u>angel</u> followed them, saying with a loud voice,* **If any man worship the beast and his image, and receive his mark in his forehead, or in his hand.**

REVELATION 14:10—**The same drink of the wine of the wrath of God, which is poured out without mixture into the cup of his indignation** (righteous anger)**; and he shall be tormented with fire and brimstone** (sulfur—which has a rotten egg odor) **in the presence of his holy <u>angels</u>, and in the presence of the Lamb.**

REVELATION 14:15—*And another <u>angel</u> came out of the temple, crying with a loud voice to him that sat on the cloud,* **Thrust in thy sickle, and reap; for the time is come for thee to reap; for the harvest of the earth is ripe.**

REVELATION 14:17—*And another* angel *came out of the temple which is in heaven, he also having a sharp sickle.*

REVELATION 14:18—*And another* angel *came out from the altar; which had power over fire; and cried with a loud cry to him that had the sharp sickle, saying,* **Thrust in thy sharp sickle, and gather the clusters of the vine of the earth; for her grapes are fully ripe.**

I do hope you are reading and studying as you go. What is this telling you? To me it is saying that those who do not follow God's commandments and do not follow Jesus, or have him in their hearts, will be gone. But those that do follow both God and Jesus, and have died, will rest from their labors, and their good works will follow them. (When they go to heaven)

Now I do believe that these angels are either destroyer angels or are captains of the angels. I do lean mostly toward the destroyer angels though.

REVELATION 15:1—*And I saw another sign in heaven, great and marvelous, seven* angels *having the seven last plagues; for in them is filled up the wrath of God.*

REVELATION 15:6—*And the seven* angels *came out of the temple, having the seven plagues, clothed in pure and white linen, and having their breasts girded with golden girdles.*

REVELATION 15:7—*And one of the four* beasts *gave unto the seven* angels *seven golden vials full of the wrath of God, who liveth for ever and ever.*

REVELATION 15:8—*And the temple was filled with smoke from the glory of God, and from his power; and no man was able to enter into the temple, till the seven plagues of the seven* angels *were fulfilled.*

REVELATION 16:1—*And I heard a great voice out of the temple saying to the seven* angels, ***Go your ways, and pour out the vials of wrath of God upon the earth.***

The next verse I am going to put down here for you, for it is the first angel that is doing this.

REVELATION 16:2—*And the first went, and poured out his vial upon the earth; and there fell a noisome* (being unpleasant as it is very dirty and has a bad odor) *and grievous* (bad, severe) *sore upon the men which had the mark of the beast, and upon them which worship his image.*

REVELATION 16:3—*And the second angel poured out his vial upon the sea; and it became as the blood of a dead man; and every living soul died in the sea.*

REVELATION 16:4—*And the third angel poured out his vial upon the rivers and fountains of waters; and they became blood.*

REVELATION 16:5—*And I heard the angel of the waters say,* **Thou art righteous, O Lord, which art, and wast,** (was) **and shalt be, because thou hast judged thus.**

REVELATION 16:8—*And the fourth angel poured out his vial upon the sun; and the power was given unto him to scorch* (burn) *men with fire.*

REVELATION 16:10—*And the fifth angel poured out his vial upon the seat of the beast; and his kingdom was full of darkness; and they gnawed* (chewed, bite on) *their tongues in pain.*

REVELATION 16:12—*And the sixth angel poured out his vial upon the great river Euphrates; and the water thereof was dried up, that the way of the kings of the east might be prepared.*

To me this means that when the kings of the east come they can follow the dried river bed to find their way.

REVELATION 16:17—*And the seventh angel poured out his vial into the air; and there came a great voice from the throne, saying,* **It is done.**

The next verse will tell of the great earthquake, and then the next verse will tell of the great city being divided with all other cities falling. Then Babylon came before God to get the cup of wine of the fierceness of his wrath. All islands fled, and mountains were no longer here. Then the hail fell unto the earth and all men left were blaspheming (swearing at; being disrespectful) the Lord, because of the hail being so large.

REVELATION 17:1—*And there came one of the seven angels which had the seven vials, and talked with me, saying unto me, Come hither; I will shew* (show) *unto you the judgment of the great whore that sitteth upon many waters;*

REVELATION 17:7—*And the* <u>angel</u> **said unto me, Wherefore didst thou marvel? I will tell thee the mystery of the woman, and of the beast that carrieth her, which hath the seven heads and ten horns.**

Now when you read all of chapter seventeen, the verses that I did not write down; are telling of the woman who is the city of Babylon, and the beasts seven heads are seven mountains for her to sit on. And there are seven kings, five are no longer, one is here and the other is yet to come. And the ten horns are ten kings, which have no kingdoms yet; and will receive their power one hour with the beast. These will declare war with the Lamb (Jesus) but the Lamb will overcome them. Also the ten horns will attack the whore as they hate her and shall make her desolate and naked, and will eat her flesh and burn her with fire.

REVELATION 18:1—*And after these things I saw another* <u>angel</u> *come down from heaven, having great power; and the earth was lightened* (reduce in unpleasantness) *with his glory.*

The rest of this chapter (eighteen) is about how Babylon will fall in one hour taking some of the wicked with her, if they already have not gone. In one more verse in this chapter it tells of an angel, which I have put next.

REVELATION 18:21—*And a mighty angel took up a stone like a great millstone, and cast it into the sea saying,* **Thus with violence shall the great city Babylon be thrown down, and shall be found no more at all.**

Then it continues to tell of the items that this city will do no more; such as the sounds of someone being married, down to no light from a candle shall be seen. Then verse twenty four mentions that the blood of the prophets, saints, and all that were slain upon the earth would be found in her.

Chapter nineteen tells of the ones in heaven proclaiming Alleluia to God, including the four beasts, which is in verse four. Then it goes on to tell of the marriage of the Lamb and his wife, then goes into the section that tells of the great white horse and the one that sat on the horse was called Faithful and True, and he judges and makes war. And the armies in heaven followed him. Then in verse seventeen it is worded as such:

REVELATION 18:17—*And I saw an angel standing in the sun; and he cried with a loud voice, saying to all the fowls that fly in the midst of heaven,* **Come and gather yourselves together unto the supper of the great God.** *(Verse 18)* **That ye may eat the flesh of kings, and the flesh of captains, and the flesh of mighty men, and the flesh of horses, and of them that sit on them, and the flesh of all men, both free and bond, both small and great.**

This is when Satan and his fallen angels and friends are defeated and it tells that some are put into the lake of fire burning with brimstone. Others were slain with the sword and then the fowls (birds) were filled with flesh from all that died. (In other words they cleaned the earth of everything that was dead.

REVELATION 20:1—*And I saw an <u>angel</u> come down from heaven, having the key of the bottomless pit and a great chain in his hand.*

Then this goes on to tell of the devil being tied up in the chain for a thousand years, and then cast into the bottomless pit, being shut up inside with a great seal upon him, then after the thousand years he will be untied to come again for a short time. The dead that believed in Jesus would live with Him, for a thousand years, but others that did not believe would wait until the first resurrection was over. (The second thousand years)

Then it goes on to tell of Satan being released and what he tries to do, and how God takes him down again, but this time he is in the bottomless pit "forever". Then all people would be judged by the Book of Life and what was written in it that book, about that person and some would go to the bottomless pit with Satan.

Now when you get into chapter twenty one, it tells of John seeing the new earth and the new heaven, and there was no sea, anymore. Then it goes on to tell of the New Jerusalem coming down from heaven, being all prepared to be the bride of Jesus. All of this I believe to be the most beautiful part of the whole Bible, from chapter twenty one through the rest of the book of Revelation. This is one more mention of an angel in this section, verse nine.

REVELATION 21:9—*And there came to me one of the seven angels which had the seven vials full of the seven last plagues, and talked with me, saying,* **Come hither, I will show thee the bride, the Lamb's wife.**

Then it tells of what the New Jerusalem will look like along with the measurements of the city. And in verse seventeen it tells of this by an angel:

And he measured the wall thereof, an hundred and forty and four cubits, (Measurement from the elbow to the end of the tip of the center finger) *according to the measure of a man, that is, of the <u>angel</u>.*

REVELATION 22:6—*And he said unto me,* **These sayings are faithful and true; and the Lord God of the holy prophets sent his <u>angel</u> to shew unto his servants the things which must shortly be done.**

You must remember that one day to God, is one thousand days for us.

Now this is the last mention of an angel in the Bible which you will find in Chapter twenty two.

REVELATION 22:16—I Jesus have sent mine <u>angel</u> to testify unto you these things in the churches, I am the root and the offspring of David, and the bright and morning star.

Now when you are finishing this last chapter in the Book of Revelation and the end of the Bible, you must read verse eighteen and nineteen, then understand it. If you cannot understand then it definitely is time to talk with your pastor or preacher or minister.

We will now start from the first book of the Bible Genesis again and will tell of the Fallen Angels and Satan. (Or the Angel of Light) I am sure it will not take too long, for God and Jesus want you to know their love and they Hope you have love for them. Think on that for a second: DO YOU HAVE LOVE FOR THEM??

Do NOT let Satan get in your heart, Worship and pray ONLY to God and his only begotten son; Jesus. Thanks.

Also in the Book of Revelation, Chapter twenty two and verse nine it says this and as I said earlier, do Not Worship Angels!! This is after John fell down to worship the angel, as the angel was telling him all about the New Jerusalem:

REVELATION 22:9—*Then saith unto me, See thine do it not; for I am thy fellow servant, and of thy brethren* (brother) *the prophets, and of them which keep the sayings of this book:* worship God.

There are also other places that tell you the same thing; do not worship angels, only worship God and his only begotten son Jesus.

Just a quick note on ANGELS:

Look in the front of this book for the list of angels (grouping) and then add the following:

Do Watchers belong with regular angels—I say no.

Put Rulers in with Principalities, Powers, and Thrones.

Look up Daniel again and put that type of angel down.

Look up Ezekiel and put that type of angel down (to me it is different than Daniels.

Then in Daniel he has a different angel near the end Clothed in Linen and gold, etc:

That would bring the total up to sixteen different types of angels.

Then the four beasts in Revelation; are they a type of angel? Why does Abaddon or Apollyon have names when other angels do not? Are they Archangels or another type of angel? (To me they are similar to our jailers that guard prisoners, and could be a separate angel).

Okay scholars what is what?

FALLEN ANGELS AND THE ANGEL OF LIGHT

Going through the Old Testament, starting with the Book of Genesis; ending in the New Testament in the Book of Revelation

I am "not" going to get very heavy into demons (Fallen angels) and Satan, as I do not want you to get too interested in them, for I want you to think more of the good angels and our Lord God and his only begotten son, Jesus.
The word Satan comes from the word Santanus (Which I believe is a Greek word) and the Aramaic word Santana.
I am going to list some of the names for Satan and where you can find them in the Bible.
Lucifer: Isaiah 14:12 (Son of the morning) or morning star. Also light bearer, or the Angel of Light.
These names that I have found below next, I do not know what book they are in; unless they are in the Catholic Bible or in books that have been taking out of the Bible as being not trustworthy:
Azazel,—Mastema
The following, I will put the book they are in down, so you can look up the names if you wish:
Beelzebul (Mark—Matthew)
Sammael (Isaiah)
Belial or Beliar (2nd Corinthians)

Devil (Matthew—Luke—John—Acts)
Evil one (Matthew—John—1st John—2nd Thessalonians)
Ruler of the Demons (Mark)
The Enemy (Matthew—Luke)
Ruler of the World (John)
Tempter (Matthew—2nd Thessalonians)

I know there are more names for Satan that I have seen in the Bible, but this old man just cannot keep remembering as it taxes my brain, and I must say that my brain is not very big.

Now Satan will disguise himself as "an angel of light" (2 Corinthians 11:14) and then will go after the Christians of the world by using Scripture itself to confuse all of the people of earth. He does not have to work on the wicked and sinful people on earth for they already belong to him; he only wants the pious (devout, religious) and unsuspecting people. So you, and I, must be on the lookout for an angel that can look like any other angel, but he will be disguised, for he is still the Devil. Yes, in the Book of Job, he has the permission from God to do what he will do to a man that is following God, to see if his love of God is true, and Satan LOST. How many other small battles Satan has lost is unknown, but there are many books out there from other religions that do have other stories in them about Satan.

Now according to some scholars they say that one third of the angels are fallen angels and follow Satan. God created them for his use, but they refused or rebelled and did not obey God. Now they follow Satan and they know their fate in the future; death or the fiery pit called hell, for eternity.

And I want you to know that I am not positive on the next item as I was not really able to check out my information, but, the Shophar {Also spelled Shofar} (Rams horn) which is blown on Rosh Hashanah to confuse Satan. Believe me, he is still out there waiting to cause havoc among the people of earth.

One other item about Satan is that he is in books of other religions as well as our Christian Bible. Satan is listed in Judaism, in the Hebrew Apocrypha, in the Talmud and other Rabbinic writing, in Islam, Yazidism, Baha'i Faith, and of course in Satanism as you should know. So if others talk of him, then HE MUST BE AMONGST US, so be careful.

We know that Jesus rid the demons from people who where possessed, and I thought I would list other places where they can be found in the next paragraph here: (I may miss a few so please forgive me if I did).

Matthew 4:24—8:16—8:28—8:33—9:32—12:22
Mark 1:32—5:16—5:18
Luke 8:27—8:36
John 7:20—8:48—8:52—10:20
Acts—19:13 through 20

Now the mention of Demons in the Bible is a fairly long list which I will put down next: (Again I may have missed a couple but please forgive this OLD man, as his file drawers in his brain are getting rusty, and stick now and then).

Deuteronomy 32:14
Psalm 106:37
Matthew 7:22—8:31—9:34—10:8—12:24—12:27—12:28
Mark 1:34—1:39—3:15—3:22—5:12—5:15—6:13—9:38—16:9—16:17
Luke 4:41—8:2—8:30—8:32—8:33—8:35—8:38—9:1—9:49—10:17—11:15—11:18—11:20—13:32
Romans 8:38
1st Corinthians 10:20—10:21
1st Timothy 4:1
James 2:19

Revelation 9:20—16:14—18:2

So if you wish to find out about demons and being possessed by demons, you have a lot of reading to do. I leave that up to you as I do not really wish you to start worshipping any fallen angels or Satan. And Satan will sure try to get you over to his side if he thinks he can hook you, so fair warning, and be very careful.

We will start on where you will find items about Satan, and what it is about, right from the Bible.

Now to me the first mention of Satan is in the Garden of Eden, but he is a serpent (snake) and tempts Eve to eat the fruit of the Tree of Good and Evil, then she gives it to Adam. You can find this in Genesis 3:1-24, and in verse 14 it will tell you what God did to the serpent or snake telling the serpent that he would go on his belly and eat dust the rest of eternity. And some scholars say that when you look at a snake and his bone structure, he has places for small legs, such as a centipede would have.

The next item it does not really say anything about Satan, but deep down inside me I believe he could have been the instigator of the murder of Abel by his brother Cain. This was the first murder in our world, and just think of how many murders there are today in this world. Even though God gave us the Ten Commandments with one being, Thou Shalt Not Kill, we just keep doing it. Now you can read about Cain and Abel in Genesis 4:1-26.

All through the Bible it tells of the people going back to worshipping other god's, and to me this is Satan trying to get the people away from God. God keeps telling the people that He is a jealous God and He will take action against those that go against Him.

This is one of the first mentions of the name of Satan in the Bible: Remember he has gone by other names as well.

1ˢᵗ CHRONICALS 21:1—*And Satan stood up against Israel, and provoked David to number Israel.*

This David new was wrong but had Joab count the people anyway, and the Lord was very displeased with David, so he punished Israel. To me it should have been only David that was punished, but the Israel people must not have been doing what was right also, so God punished them.

We will go to the book of Job and find Satan there: Here is a Godly man with seven sons and three daughters, some wealth, and was well liked. God was very pleased with Job and Satan said to God that he could take Job away from God, but failed. This book is a MUST read for all of you, and I want you to take your time reading it and understanding what you do read. There are two questions I have for you, one is,—Can "you" do what Job did during Satan's way of dealing with Job to get him away from God? After it was all over, would you still be with God? If I was a betting man, I would say maybe one out of one hundred would stay with God, the rest would be angry with him. What do YOU think?

JOB 1:6—*Now there was a day when the sons of God* (angels) *came to present themselves before the Lord, and Satan came also among them.*

JOB 1:7—*And the Lord said unto Satan,* **Whence comest thou?** *Then Satan answered the Lord, and said, From going to and fro in the earth, and from walking up and down in it.*

JOB 1:8—*And the Lord said unto Satan,* **Hast thou considered my servent Job, that there is none like him in the earth, a perfect and an upright man, one that feareth God, and eschewith** (avoid, shun) **evil?**

JOB 1:9—*Then Satan answered the Lord, and said, Doth* (does) *Job fear God for nought* (nothing)?

Just read verses ten and eleven, if you would please.

JOB 1:12—*And the Lord said unto Satan,* **Behold, all that he hath is in thy power; only upon himself put not forth thy hand.** *So Satan went forth from the presence of the Lord.*

God is so sure that Job will remain with him he is letting Satan do what he wishes, but cannot do harm to Job himself. Now as you read you see all that is happening to Job and his family, and yet he still worships God. Do you think that you could worship and praise God after losing all you children and livelihood? I have had my ups and downs over the years and I still worship at least two times a day. It should be more, I know that, but the hustle and bustle of the world today makes it a little awkward.

JOB 2:1—*Again there was a day when the sons of God came to present themselves before the Lord, and Satan came also among them to present himself before the Lord.*

JOB 2:2—*And the Lord said unto Satan,* **From whence cometh thou?** *And Satan answered the Lord, and said, From going to and fro in the earth, and from walking up and down on it.*

JOB 2:3—*And the Lord said unto Satan,* **Hast thou considered my servant Job, that there is none like him in the earth, a perfect and an upright man, one that feareth God, and escheweth** (avoid, shun) **evil? And still he hodeth fast his integrity** (honor)**, although thou movedst me against him, to destroy him without cause.**

JOB 2:4—*And Satan answered the Lord, and said, yea, all that a man hath will he give for his life.*

JOB 2:5—*But put forth thine hand now, and touch his bone and his flesh, and he will curse thee to thy face.*

JOB 2:6—*And the Lord said unto Satan,* **Behold, he is in thine hand, but save his life.**

JOB 2:7—*So went Satan forth from the presence of the Lord, and smote* (struck) *Job with sore boils from the sole of his foot unto his crown* (head).

JOB 2:8—*And he took him a potsherd* (piece of broken pottery) *to scrape himself withal; and he sat down among the ashes.*

JOB 2:9—*Then said his wife unto him, Dost thou still retain thine integrity? Curse God, and die.*

All I can say about his wife, is she is not very nice to Job, telling him to curse God and die. Of course the Devil probably had something to do with her talking like that. Those are divorce words, in our life today.

JOB 2:10—*But he said unto her, Thou speakest as one of the foolish women speaketh. What? Shall we receive good at the hand of God, and shall we not receive evil? In all this did not Job sin with his lips.*

Now when you read the rest of Job, you will find Job feeling sorry for himself, and three of his friends are with him. They talk to one another, such as Job talking then one of the three will talk. Near the end God talks to all of them and gives Job's friends another chance, IF Job prays for them, and offers a sacrifice for each, which Job does and his friends are forgiven. Job never condemns God and is given everything back, better than when Satan has taken everything from him. Now, as Job does his talking, which are similar to a parable, he tells another scientific fact that took us centuries to find out. If you read all of Job, you had to have read it. Look up Job 26:7 and read this item; (I will only put the second half here for you).

And hangeth the earth upon nothing.

If you can remember, that the ancients pictured earth on the shoulders of a god or someone like Hercules is the way they believed. How else would the earth stay where it was? This shows that the earth hung from nothing in the sky. Keep reading—maybe you will discover something that has been missed all these years.

This next item is a Psalm, and I want you to read this entire Psalm; actually you should read all of the Psalms, slowly, and understand what is written. I am only putting down the part that refers to Satan.

PSALM 109:6—*Set thou a wicked man over him; and let Satan stand at his right hand.*

As you read this Psalm I think you will get the idea that David had a lot of adversaries (Opponent), and he is praying to God to help him against these adversaries. He is actually telling God what to do with these people, which to me is not the best way. To me I would ask for some type of punishment for them, but not to tell God what to do.

Now we will go into the book of Zechariah. When you read this book, I want you to read slowly so you will understand each chapter and verse therein.

ZACHARIAH 3:1& 2—*And he showed me Joshua the high priest standing before the angel of the Lord, and Satan standing at his right hand to resist him. (2) And the Lord said unto Satan,* **The Lord rebuke thee, O Satan; even the Lord that hath chosen Jerusalem rebuke thee; is not this a brand plucked out of the fire?**

That is all I could find on Satan in this book, but he has been rebuked by God, for his misdeeds. Then when you get to verse eight of this same chapter you will find the word BRANCH. This is Zechariah referring to someone that the Lord will bring forth to them. From what I have dug up in literature, is this word does have more than one meaning, but here it means the person is both a priest and a king. Now it could be the angel talking to Zechariah, but the way it is worded it could be the Lord talking to him. Now in Chapter 6, verse 12 it will say this: "saying, Behold the man whose name is THE BRANCH; and he shall grow up out of his place, and he shall build the temple of the Lord". As I think on this, is it to signify that Jesus IS coming, and will be both a priest and king over Israel? A good one, for our scholars to come up with an answer, that is a good answer and not lead us in circles. But maybe it was Solomon, or someone that was from that area after Solomon. I will let them decide. AHHH, such mysteries the Bible holds.

Let us go to the Book of Matthew (A Gospel).

Again I am not putting everything down as I hope you can read by now, just take your time and understand what you are reading. If you have a problem or problems, see or talk to either your pastor or a Bible study leader. Most of the dealing with Satan is in chapter four and I will try to cover it the best I can for you to learn from. Now in this chapter Satan will be listed as the Devil and the tempter.

MATTHEW 4: 1-11—*Then when Jesus led up of the spirit into the wilderness to be tempted of the devil.*

MATTHEW 4:3—*And when the tempter came to him, he said, If thou be the Son of God, command that these stones be made bread.*

MATTHEW 4:5—*Then the devil taketh him up into the holy city, and setteth him on a pinnacle* (highest point) *of the temple.*

MATTHEW 4:8—*Again the devil taketh him up into an exceeding high mountain, and sheweth him all the kingdoms of the world, and the gory of them;*

MATTHEW 4:11—*Then the devil leaveth him, and behold, angels came and ministered unto him.*

Just read everything in-between what I have down above, mainly to learn how Jesus answered Satan, and how he won this battle against Satan.

Now in chapter 12, verse 22 it starts talking of one possessed by the devil and I want you to read from here through the rest of this chapter, very slowly; it will tell you what you can say to whom and not to the Holy Spirit (God). Here the name of Satan will be Beelzebub, the prince of the devils.

MATTHEW 16:23—*But he turned, and said unto Peter, Get behind me, Satan: thou art an offence unto me, for thou savorest not the things that be of God, but those that be of men.*

This is one time in the Bible that Jesus reprimands one of his disciples and calls him Satan. It is like he knew that Satan was putting those words into Peter's mouth. Read all of this slowly so you can understand what is going on.

Now we will look at Chapter 25 verse 41, this is when Jesus says this to his disciples: What you have done for the thirsty, the hungry, you have done unto me.

MATTHEW 25:41—*Then shall he say also unto them on the left hand, Depart from me, ye cursed, unto everlasting fire. Prepared for the devil and his angels.*

If you pardon my swearing here, just for a moment: It is a nice way of saying, Go to Hell. This finishes the book of Matthew and what it says about Satan. We will now travel into the book of Mark, another Gospel.

Mark is the second book of the New Testament, and is the second Gospel. This is what he mentions about Satan.

MARK 1:13—*And he was there in the wilderness forty days, tempted of Satan; and was with the wild beasts; and the angels ministered unto him.*

To find out more you would have to go back to Matthew and read the same part in that book, as Mark does not mention Satan much here, and what happened during those forty days.

Now this is a Parable of Jesus dealing with the sower (planting) of the word. It is worded as such in my KJV Bible.

MARK 4:15—*And these are they by the way side, where the word is sown; but when they have heard, Satan cometh immediately, and taketh away the word that was sown in their hearts.*

This is just mentioning that no matter who sows the word, if they are truly not believers, Satan will take that word from them, and will confuse these people. I do believe that is all there is on Satan, in the book of Mark.

Now we will go to the book of Luke and see what he has to offer about Satan. Now this Gospel of Luke (third Gospel) is a lot like Matthew in some respects. Someday I want to work with all four Gospels and see just what the differences are between each book with all subjects written.

LUKE 4:1-13—*And Jesus being full of the Holy Ghost returned from Jordon, and was led by the Spirit into the wilderness, (2) Being forty days tempted of the devil. And in those days he did eat nothing; and when they were ended, he afterward hungered. (3) And the devil said unto him, if thou be the son of God, command this stone that it be made bread.*

LUKE 4:5—*And the devil, taking him up into an high mountain, showed unto him all the kingdoms of the world in a moment of time. (6) And the devil said unto him, All this power will I give thee, and the glory of them; for that is delivered unto me; and to whomsoever I will I give it. (7) If thou therefore wilt* (will) *worship me, all shall be thine.* (8) *And Jesus answered and said unto him, Get thee behind me, Satan: for it is written, Thou shalt worship the Lord thy God, and him only shalt thou serve.* (9) *And he (Satan) brought him (Jesus) to Jerusalem, and set him on a pinnacle of the temple, and said unto him, If thou shalt be the Son of God, cast thyself down from hence:* (10) *For it is written, he shall give his angels charge over thee, to keep thee:* (11) *And in their hands they shall bear thee up, lest at any time thou dash thy foot against a stone.* (12) *And Jesus answering said unto him, It is said, Thou shalt not tempt the Lord thy God.* (13) *And when the devil had ended all the temptation, he departed from him for a season* (period of time).

<u>LUKE 10:17,18,19</u>—(17) *And the seventy* (these are apostles that Jesus sent out two by two) *returned again with joy, saying, Lord, even the devils are subject unto us through thy name.* (18) *And he said unto them, I beheld Satan as lightning falling from heaven.* (19) *Behold, I give unto you power to tread on serpents and scorpions, and over all the power of the enemy: and nothing shall by any means hurt you.*

In this part of Luke it does not say a lot about Satan, and Jesus is talking to his apostles telling them that Satan is no longer (or will be no longer) in heaven.

<u>LUKE 11:15</u>—*But some of them said, He casteth out devils* (demons) *through Beelzebub the chief of the devils.*

<u>LUKE 11:18</u>—(This is Jesus talking) *If Satan also be divided against himself, how shall his kingdom stand? Because ye say that I cast out devils through Beelzebub.* (19) *And if I by Beelzebub cast out devils, by whom do your sons cast them out? Therefore shall they be your judges.*

Hopefully you are reading all around what I have put down here, for Satan's kingdom would be divided if Beelzebub was different from the demons and Satan. Then there would be two Devils to worry about.

LUKE 22:3—(This is when Judas goes to the priests and gets money to betray Jesus.) *Then entered Satan into Judas surnamed Iscariot, being of the number of the twelve.*

And as you read Judas betrays Jesus with a kiss, at the Mount of Olives. Now Satan is mentioned again in this same chapter, but in verse thirty one. This is how it is worded.

LUKE 22:31—*And the Lord said, Simon, Simon, behold, Satan hath desired to have you, that he may sift you as wheat.*

This is just a short item that I nearly missed reading too fast years ago. Jesus goes on to say more, but I want you to know that Satan was after Simon as well as others, but Jesus prayed hard for him and Simon went on and continued his teaching. So never think that Satan will leave you alone, he could be lurking around the next doorway.

Now in John (The last of the Gospels written), I do know you will find the word devil a few times but to me they are meant as devil possessed. I do not remember seeing the word Satan in this book, but if you do find one, it is okay to yell at me. I know I am not perfect (just "beeauuutiful"). Woops, no conceit in my family, I have it all.

ROMANS 16:20—(This is the only mention of Satan in this book, which I know of: but prove me wrong) *And the God of peace shall bruise Satan under your feet shortly. The grace of our Lord Jesus Christ be with you. Amen.*

This is just saying that God will take care of Satan when it is time, and it will be at a time so that you will know it is going on. (I have decided you need a little break—Go get yourself a cup of coffee or whatever, sit back and enjoy a couple of Jokes I have inserted for you to enjoy).

This one deals with Hitler, Satan, and Jesus.

Hitler finds himself at the front door of Hell. So he knocks and Satan opens the door, and asks who he is. So he replies Adolf Hitler, and Satan is flabbergasted, saying I know what you did on earth, and there is no way you are coming into Hell, go see Jesus. So Hitler goes up to heaven and knocks on the pearly gates of Heaven, thinking this is great after all the things I have done and I am sent up here. The next day there is a knock on the door to Hell again and Satan answers and finds Jesus standing there, with Satan asking why he is there. Jesus answers him: I just escaped from "Stalag Heaven" and want to apply for political asylum.

Okay, just one more, than back to this book you are reading.

One bright early morning, everyone in town gets up and goes to the town church for their Sunday service. But before the service starts they are all talking about their week and what is going on in their lives. SUDDENLY, by the alter Satan appears and everyone starts running and screaming and Satan just stands their laughing. Shortly everyone has left the church except one older man sitting in a pew near the front. This puzzles Satan as why he did not run, so he asks the man; Are you not afraid of me? And you do know who I am, do you not? The man looks at Satan and says, Yes, I know who you are, and no I am not frightened of you, because I married your sister thirty five years ago.

Okay enough of these stupid jokes, for you see, I cannot tell a good joke most of the time. I usually goof them up somewhere. Okay back to the book.

1st CORINTHIANS 5:5—This is an Epistle to the Corinthians by Paul and Satan is just mentioned in this verse.—*To deliver such an one unto Satan for the destruction of the flesh, that the spirit, may be saved in the day of the Lord Jesus.*

Now as you read the rest of this book; 1st Corinthians, you will come across a word which is in chapter 12 verse 25 and I know that a lot of people will scratch their head over this word. This word is the word "schism" so I will give you a few definitions here: Split, break, division, and rift. Has your church gone through this? Did it work okay for everyone, or were their problems? For this is Satan trying to divide and conquer, so be careful, for he is always around looking for a small opening to attack from.

We will jump over to the Epistle of Paul's which is the second one to the Corinthians; this is what it says about Satan:

2nd CORINTHIANS 11:14,15—(I have decided to add verse 13 in here as well)

Verse 13—*For such are false apostles, deceitful workers, transforming themselves into the apostles of Christ.*

Verse 14—*And no marvel; for Satan himself is transformed into an angel of light.*

Verse 15—*Therefore it is no great thing if his ministers also are transformed as the ministers of righteousness; whose end shall be according to their works.*

2nd CORINTHIANS 12:7—*And lest I should be exalted above measure through the abundance of the revelations, there was given to me a thorn in the flesh, the messenger of Satan to buffet me, lest I should be exalted above measure.*

I do hope you are reading all of these Epistles and letters that Paul has written, as it will tell you of some of the things he has had to go through to be an Apostle of Christ's. Also dealing with what other people should look for to keep Satan from our door. There is one item I would like you to especially take note of which is in one of the next verses: Verse 10—*Therfore I take pleasure in infirmities, in reproaches, in* *necessities, in persecutions, in distress for Christ's sake: <u>for when I am weak, then am I strong.</u>*

If you are working for God or his only son Jesus Christ, and it seems like you cannot go on any more, and you feel like giving up, that is when Satan is trying to draw you away from the Lord God and Jesus. So just keep going, you will get the strength to endure all that is bothering you.

We will look at Galatians and see what we can find, for you to learn from:

GALATIONS 5:16-21—*This I say then, Walk in the Spirit, and ye shall not fulfill the lust* (desire) *of the flesh. (17) For the flesh lusteth against the spirit, and the spirit against the flesh, and these are contrary the one to the other; so that ye cannot do the things that ye would. (18) But if ye be led of the Spirit, ye are not under the law, (19) Now the works of the flesh are manifest* (obvious), *which are these; Adultery*(cheating on spouse), *fornication* (immoral sexual behavior), *uncleanness* (Religiously impure), *lasciviousness* (sexually interested in an unpleasant way), *(20) Idolatry* (worshiping idols), *witchcraft* (practicing magic for evil purposes), *hatred, variance* (inconsistency), *emulations* (try to be better or equal to God), *wrath* (vengeance), *strife* (trouble), *seditions*(to provoke or incite rebellion), *heresies*(action to oppose religion or God). *(21) Envyings* (to be resentful of other people's success), *murders, drunkenness, reveling* (partying), *and such like; of which I tell you before, as I have also told you in time past, that they which do such things <u>shall not</u> inherit the kingdom of God.*

To me this is Satan (flesh) fighting God (Spirit). I know a lot of people may disagree with me on this, but I do not care, this is how I look at this section of the bible. It does say "the works of the flesh", and then goes on to list a lot of items that the Devil would, and will, try to get you away from God. Has the Devil gotten to you yet? Have you done any of these items? Are you still doing them? Have you changed your ways? If you are still doing these things and do not intend to repent, I guess a lot of people will see "you" in the Bottomless pit called Hell. The following you will find in the book of Ephesians.

EPHESIANS 6:11—*Put on the whole armor of God, that ye may be able to stand against the wiles* (strategy) *of the devil.*

EPHESIANS 6:12—*For we wrestle not against flesh and blood, but against principalities, against powers, against the rulers of the darkness of this world, against spiritual wickedness in high places.*

The rest of this chapter deals with putting on the armor of God. Now I hope that you recognized that the principalities and powers in this verse are listed as evil. Remember, some scholars think they are good, and here in the King James Version they are considered evil, so where do they sometimes get their information? Although when I read chapter 1:21, it is telling me; that they may be good, this is how it is worded:

EPHESIANS 1:21—*Far above all principalities, and power, and might, and dominion, and every name that is named, not only in this world, but in that which is to come; (22) And hath put all things under his feet, and gave him to be the head over all things to the church.*

This is just saying that Jesus will put all these things under himself and he will be in charge of them, in this world and in heaven. As I have said many times, the Bible can be confusing and a lot of people will be lost when they just read the Bible; "You have to study as you read". I do admit that I am confused a lot (even when I am not reading the Bible) and this could be, that Jesus will take them away from Satan, and will use them himself, and will be king over them. Now I may skip some books as I cannot remember seeing anything about Satan (or the devil) listed in them. But just check them out as it will be good studying for YOU.

Another Epistle of Paul's to the Colossians, and this is the only mention of Satan that I remember and it is not worded as Satan. Just read it and you will find out what I am talking about.

COLOSSIANS 1:13—*Who hath delivered us from the power of darkness, and hath translated us into the kingdom of his dear Son.*

I do hope that you saw that Satan is the "power of darkness". He goes by many names, and you may even have one for him as well.

This next Epistle of Paul's is the First Epistle to Timothy: and I believe there is only one place that mentions Satan.

1st TIMOTHY 1:20—*Of whom is Hymenaeus and Alexander; whom I have delivered unto Satan, that they may learn not to blaspheme* (Curse, swear, insult religion).

So just be careful to not swear or do any type of insulting of any church. I know a lot of people will knock down one religion saying bad things about them. Satan loves them, so do not do it if you do not care to be with Satan in the future.

This is from the Epistle of James and is just one verse that says anything about the devil or Satan.

JAMES 4:7—*Submit yourselves therefore to God. Resist the devil, and he will flee from you.*

As you are reading I hope that you have been paying some attention to what is written and how it is written. To me it is getting easier to read for the language is more easily understood. It seems to be coming up into our style, a long way off yet, but getting better.

We now go into the First Epistle of Peter, and again there is only one verse that I know of that pertains to Satan or the devil.

1st PETER 5:8—*Be sober, be vigilant; because your adversary the devil, as a roaring lion, walketh about, seeking whom he may devour.*

I hope I never get devoured by him in this life, and if I come back again I hope that he will be gone forever.

Now as we go into the books of John, or the Epistles of John there is only one place that mention the devil, and I thought since these three books are very small you can read them and find it yourself. But I do want you to also find what he says about the antichrist that will come before Satan try's to take over the world. Hopefully you are not trying to do this, to be an antichrist, against the church or Jesus.

Now there is only one more book for you to read which is: the Epistle of Jude and it is a very small book, so it will only take a minute or two. Just study it as you read, for there are items in there, which I would like you to learn about. They deal with the fallen angels and the cities that God destroyed. This is the only item that mentions the devil:

JUDE 1:9—*Yet, Michael the archangel, when contending with the devil he disputed about the body of Moses, durst* (dare) *not bring against him a railing accusation, but said, The Lord rebuke* (reprimand) *thee.*

I do pray that after reading the entire Bible up to this point, you have learned new items that you did not know before. A lot is to be learned and our lives are very short, so the quicker you learn the better it will be for you, TRUST ME.

Okay, I have given you enough time to check out the book of Romans and see if you could prove me wrong. This is not really mentioning the devil (or Satan), but does mention what is written next.

It is Romans 1:25—*Who changed the truth of God into a lie, and worshipped and served the creature more than the Creator, who is blessed for ever. Amen.*

So I did not lie to you as it truly does not say Satan or the devil, but here he is called the <u>creature</u>. So you do have to read slowly if you did not catch this, and study as you read,—okay; okay. Little verses like this you can miss very easily, as I believe a lot of people may be more interested in what comes next as it goes into those who are unrighteous, maliciousness, wickedness, covetousness, fornicate, full of envy, murder, deceit, whisperers, haters of God, inventors of evil things, disobedient. It also brings up homosexuality, and that is why I think you should really study this book, all the way through it. I do not condemn those that are led down that path (by Satan) as that is for our Lord to do. Some have even murdered homosexuals, saying it is what God wants, but they have forgotten all of the Ten Commandments by God and the two from Jesus. There are a few places in the Bible that states that homosexuality is a sin, but I do not remember the Bible saying how we should do away with these people. "That will be up to God".

Now we will go into the last book of the Bible, the Book of Revelation and will study the devil and or Satan, whichever one you wish to call him. Now Paul is in heaven with the angels and Jesus and God; and we will start with a letter that Paul is to write to the angel of the church of Smyrna. The best way for me to explain all of this is if you take the time to read and study the book of Revelation, but I think it would be good to study it with someone that knows this book well; like a pastor or a Bible study teacher. For me to explain on paper it would take too long and you would probably miss a very important part. At least you know where it tells of Satan in this book.

REVELATION 2:9-15—(Now this is Jesus talking to Paul in heaven) *I know thy works, and tribulation and poverty, (but thou art rich) and I know the blasphemy of them which say they are Jews, and are not, but are the synagogue of Satan. (10) Fear none of these things which thou shalt suffer; behold, the devil shall cast some of you into prison, that ye may be tried; and ye shall have tribulation ten days; be thou faithful unto death, and I will give thee a crown of life. (11) He that hath an ear, let him hear what the spirit saith unto the churches; He that overcometh shall not be hurt of the second death. (12) And to the angel of the church in Pergamos write; These things saith he which hath the sharp sword with two edges. (13) I know thy works, and where thou dwellest, even where Satan's seat is: and thou holdest fast my name, and hast not denied my faith, even in those days wherein Antipas was my faithful martyr, who was slain among you, where Satan dwelleth.*

REVELATION 2:24—This is a letter to the angel of the church in Thyatira. Jesus first talks of the woman Jezebel, and then in this verse it tells of Satan, but only tells of him. *But unto you I say, and unto the rest in Thyatira, as many as have not this doctrine, and which have not know the depths of Satan, as they speak; I will put upon you none other burden.*

REVELATION 12:7-9—And *there was a war in heaven: Michael and his angels fought against the dragon; and the dragon fought and his angels, (8) And prevailed not; neither was their place found any more in heaven. (9) And the great dragon was cast out, that old serpent, called the Devil, and Satan, which deceiveth the whole world: he was cast out into the earth, and his angels were cast out with him.*

I do hope that you really do not need any help with these passages from the Bible; but I will put it down as simply as I can. Satan and all his fallen angels were thrown out of heaven and now reside on earth, or behind it, or in it. So you must still be careful, for he is looking for new people to conquer.

REVELATION 12:13-17—*And when the dragon saw that he was cast unto the earth, he persecuted the woman which brought forth the man child. (14) And the woman were given two wings of a great eagle, that she might fly into the wilderness, into her place, where she in nourished for a time, and times, and a half a time, from the face of the serpent. (15) And the serpent cast out of his mouth water as a flood after the woman, that he might cause her to be carried away of the flood. (16) And the earth helped the woman, and the earth opened her mouth, and swallowed up the flood which the dragon cast out of his mouth. (17) And the dragon was wroth with the woman, and went to make war with the remnant of her seed, which keep the commandments of God, and have the testimony of Jesus Christ.*

To me this is just saying that the woman is really all the people of earth, and her seed is all of us on earth today, that believe in God and his only begotten son, Jesus Christ.

REVELATION 13:8-18—Now this chapter starts out talking about the dragon, that brought forth the beasts, and what the beasts will do to us the people of earth. I want you to read all of chapter thirteen and really keep your mind open to other verses before what I put down, especially verse four.— (8) *And all that dwell upon the earth shall worship him, whose names are not written in the book of life of the Lamb slain* with the foundation of the world. *(9) If any man have an ear, let him hear, (10) He that leadeth into captivity shall go into capitivity; he that killeth with the sword must be killed by the sword. Here is the patience and the faith of the saints. (11) And I beheld another beast coming up out of the earth; and he had two horns like a lamb, and he spake as a dragon. (12) And he exerciseth all the power of the first beast before him, and causeth the earth and them which dwell therein to worship the first beast, whose deadly wound was healed. (13) And he doeth great wonders, so that he maketh fire come down from heaven on the earth in the sight of men. (14) And deceiveth them that dwell on the earth by the means of those miricles which he had power to do in the sight of the beast; saying to them that dwell on the earth, that they should make an image to the beast, which had the wound by a sword, and did live. (15) And he had power to give life unto the image of the beast, that the image of the beast should both speak, and cause that as many as would not worship the image of the beast should be killed. (16) And he causeth all, both small and great, rich and poor, free and bond, to receive a mark in their right hand, or in their foreheads: (17) And that no man might buy or sell, save he that had the mark, or the name of the beast, or the number of his name. (18) Here is wisdom. Let him that hath understanding count the number of the beast: for it is the number of a man; and his number is Six hundred threescore* (same as sixty) *and six.*

In other words everyone that worships Satan will have a number stamped on the hand or forehead, which is the number 666. In his world you can only buy or sell if you have that number, so if no number you would not be able to buy food for yourself or your children, etc. Satan would control everything and everybody (if he could). But as you read next, Jesus and a hundred and forty four thousand stood on Mt. Sion all having his Father's name written in their foreheads. And this is the start of the end of Satan, for a thousand years. Also it will tell of the fall of Babylon, so just keep reading, SLOWLY.

REVELATION 20:1-3—*And I saw an angel come down from heaven, having the key of the bottomless pit and a great chain in his hand. (2) And he laid hold of the great dragon, that old serpent, which is the Devil, and Satan, and bound him a thousand years, (3) And cast him into the bottomless pit, and shut him up, and set a seal upon him, that he should deceive the nations no more, till the thousand years should be fulfilled: and after that he must be loosed a little season* (Period of time).

So this is the end of Satan for a period of time of a thousand years, but then he will come back for a short period of time to again run rampant, but then he will be gone forever, which is in the next verses that I have put down for you to study.

REVELATION 20:7-10—*And when the thousand years are expired, Satan shall be loosed out of his prison, (8) And shall go out to deceive the nations which are in the four quarters of the earth, Gog and Magog* (These are listed as an enemy of God, see note below), *to gather them together to battle: the number of whom is as the sands of the sea. (9) And they went up on the breadth of the earth, and compassed the camp of the saints about, and the beloved city: and fire came down from God out of heaven and devoured them. (10) And the devil that deceived them was cast into the lake of fire and brimstone, where the beast and the false prophet are, and shall be tormented day and night for ever and ever.*

NOTE: From Verse eight above. Gog and Magog, according to some scholars, are just not positive what, or who they are, or just where they are from. One item I read said that Magog is the son of Japeth, but is also listed as a country, a person, or an ancestor. "This is something the scholars have to come up with a definition all can identify with". I know somebody is going to say, who is Japeth, well go all the way back to Noah and you will find he is one of Noah's sons who settled in the land north of the Mediterranean Sea. So Magog or Gog could be from that region (as a people or a person, but it could be the name of the land)

Now jump to verses fourteen and fifteen for the finish of this chapter. Remember to read all of it and in between these verses above and here below.

(14) *And death and hell were cast into the lake of fire. This is the second death.* (15) *And whosoever was not found written in the book of life was cast into the lake of fire.*

Congratulations: You have gone through the Bible two times, and I hope each time you have learned more of your Bible. I do believe if that you really want to, you can dive into a lot of things in the Bible and will still be amazed at what you study and read each time you open this Great Book, which I think is the Greatest Piece Of Literature Ever Written.

Thank You for your time and patience. Remember God loves you and always will if you read and understand what you read, as they are **His** words and **Jesus Christ's** words as well. AMEN.

Would you like to see your manuscript become a book?

If you are interested in becoming a PublishAmerica author, please submit your manuscript for possible publication to us at:

mybook@publishamerica.com

You may also mail in your manuscript to:

**PublishAmerica
PO Box 151
Frederick, MD 21705**

www.publishamerica.com